Mark Guy Pearse

Daniel Quorm and his religious notions

Mark Guy Pearse

Daniel Quorm and his religious notions

ISBN/EAN: 9783337262181

Printed in Europe, USA, Canada, Australia, Japan

Cover: Foto ©Lupo / pixelio.de

More available books at **www.hansebooks.com**

DANIEL QUORM,

AND HIS RELIGIOUS NOTIONS.

There, bending over his lapstone, hammering, stitching, always busy, sat Brother Dan'el; ever, too, with a book before him.—*See p. 3.*

DANIEL QUORM,

AND

HIS RELIGIOUS NOTIONS.

BY

MARK GUY PEARSE,

AUTHOR OF "MISTER HORN AND HIS FRIENDS," ETC.

ILLUSTRATED BY CHARLES TRESIDDER.

FIFTH THOUSAND.

London:
WESLEYAN CONFERENCE OFFICE,
2, CASTLE STREET, CITY-ROAD;
SOLD AT 66, PATERNOSTER ROW.
1875.

LONDON:
PRINTED BY HAYMAN BROTHERS AND LILLY,
10, CROSS ST., HATTON GARDEN, E.C.

To My Father,

WHOSE LIFE HAS MOST ENDEARED

ALL THAT IS TRUEST

AND BRIGHTEST AND BEST

IN THESE PAGES,

I DEDICATE THIS BOOK.

PREFACE.

My old friend DANIEL QUORM, of Penwinnin, is a good specimen of one service that Methodism has rendered to this country, a service that of late has come to be more generally acknowledged. In all the Methodist system there perhaps is nothing that has aided her more than her power to develop the gifts of her lowliest members; finding some sphere in which to turn to advantage the various abilities of her people. The thoughtful miner, the prayerful ploughman, the godly labourer, the working men of every class have always been amongst her most successful Leaders and Local-preachers. In hundreds of towns and villages, men of the humblest position are doing the highest work of the Church, in the Sunday-school, in the Pulpit, and in the Society-class.

The scantiest acquaintance with Methodism makes one familiar with many such. Who that has read anything of this people but has heard of Silas Told the slaver's boy, and his work at Newgate; or who has not been stirred up to start afresh by the story of the good Carvosso? Who has not heard of the village philosopher, Samuel Drew, mending shoes and working out his thoughts upon the immortality of the soul; of him who as a prince had power with God and men and prevailed,—the village blacksmith, Sammy Hick; of Billy Dawson, the wonderful Yorkshire farmer, who could sway the people like the summer breeze that swept over his own golden corn, whose words could play with cloud and sunshine across the listening hosts, and who, thrusting in the sickle, saw hundreds of sheaves gathered safely for the Lord with shouts of harvest home; of the Lincolnshire thrasher, dear good old Richardson, who could so deftly ply the flail in the service of the Heavenly Master? The ranks even of the ministry—in this like the Church of Rome—have been perhaps most richly adorned by men of humble origin.

Dan'el's beloved mother Methodism is much troubled just now by a host of physicians who would persuade her that she is ill. Some have written learned prescriptions for her in proper professional form. Many others shake their heads with gloomy foreboding and prescribe their home-made remedies, foretelling her speedy decease unless she will swallow their simples. They say that she has lost her vigour, (she used to get up at five in the morning)—that her mind is not so clear as it was, that her tongue is getting out of order, that her heart suffers from weakness if not from actual disease. Some say that she wraps herself up more than she did, has a daintier appetite and takes too much care of herself; others, that she is not particular enough with whom she associates, and that she should live more as becomes her very respectable position; others talk of old age, that her sight is growing dim, her hand becoming feeble, and her natural force abated.

Bless her, the dear old mother! why if she had not more common-sense than many of her physicians she would have taken to her bed and made her last will and testament. Let her alone. She wants from her children, not the presumption that wearies her with good advice, but their hearty love, their confidence, and their devotion. Let her alone—give her only room for plenty of exercise, and let her sons cleave to her good old-fashioned ways—to the old-fashioned simple faith in Christ, the old-fashioned entire consecration to God, the old-fashioned burning love for souls—and her most glorious days are yet to come. She knows, as well as ever she did, how to use the talents that God entrusts her with, and cares very little about position or rank or wealth so long as her sons can wield with a strong arm the hammer of the Word. She has an unwithered faith in the Sword of the Spirit. Some perhaps may daintily inscribe it with chaste ornamentation; some may set it with flashing diamonds and costly work; some may enrich it with golden hilt, and labour to make it glisten with an exquisite polish, and she thanks God for these "cunning workmen;" but she holds them as worth very little who cannot grasp it with a mighty grasp, and with a keen eye and a quick hand thrust it up to the hilt and force the enemies to cry for mercy in the dust.

Contents.

		PAGE
I.	Brother Quorm	1
II.	The Old Clock	8
III.	"My Mother's Bible"	15
IV.	Brother Quorm's Prejudice	25
V.	Brother Quorm at Class	30
VI.	Brother Dan'el on "Slow and Sure"	37
VII.	"It's the Lord's Will, you know"	42
VIII.	"Catchin' 'em with guile"	57
IX.	"Prayin' breath is never spent in vain"	62
X.	"A talk to the Lambs"	72
XI.	"Trustin' Him where we cannot trace Him"	83
XII.	Dan'el's Notion of a Class-meeting	103
XIII.	Dan'el's Notions about Searching the Scriptures	112
XIV.	On Two Ways to Heaven	128
XV.	On Winning Souls	144
XVI.	On Hearing the Word	157

DANIEL QUORM.

I.

Brother Quorm.

MY old friend Daniel Quorm,— Brother Dan'el, as he was always called — was the village shoemaker, the Methodist "Class-leader," and the "Society-steward." As hard-headed as the rounded lap-stone on which he hammered all day long, as sharp and quick as his shining awl, as obstinate in holding his own as his seasoned shoe-leather; yet, withal, Brother Dan'el had a heart so kind, so wise, so true, that like the hammer it only beat to do good, and like his awl and thread it was always trying to strengthen some poor soul that had got worn in the rough ways of life. By some process not yet discovered, the very tools that lay about him had come somehow to partake of their master's character.

Dan'el lived in the village of Penwinnin, a cluster of miners' cottages some three miles from the Circuit-town; nor would it be difficult to trace in a hundred features of the place all the chief points that struck one about Brother Dan'el.

You passed high heaps of stones on either side the way, the refuse of the mine workings, giving to all a wild and desolate look. You stepped across little streaming rivulets that had just been pumped from great depths and were yet warm. (Our poor world has a heart in it, they say. Alas! that it should be so far down.) You went under clanking chains, that stretched from the engine-house away to the shaft, and thence down in the mysterious gloom. You met men dressed in suits of flannel stained a dull ochreish red, with a candle hanging from the shoulder, and another stuck in front of the hard canvas hat, ready to light them on their perilous journey.

Now and then there were breaks in these stony heaps and one caught a glimpse of the steep cairn that rose beyond, purple with heather and brilliant with the fragrant furze, and, like an old weather-beaten castle, a pile of granite rocks crowned the summit. Or else on the other side, the break gave a peep at the valley and its red river, winding its way to the blue Atlantic that stretched beyond the headland.

Everybody in the place could tell you where Dan'el Quorm lived. You reached the little thatched cottage, crowned by luxuriant masses of the yellow stone-wort, and all girt about with fuchsias, while the dainty little "Mother-of-millions" crept over the stone fence that enclosed it. Here, without board or writing, a hundred "signs" proclaimed the shoemaker's. The window-sash was filled with all that belongs to the art and mystery of cobbling, while in the seat below were crowded odds and ends in that confusion which is dear to the true worker, let proverbial philosophy say what it will. There were the lasts and awls, the heel-taps and leather parings, the hobnails and sprigs, the cobbler's wax, and that mysterious half of a cocoa-nut shell with the little bit of grease that never got more or less.

There, bending over his lapstone, hammering, stitching, always busy, sat Brother Dan'el; ever, too, with a book before him. We could almost guess its title, for the stock is limited, and the reading is a slow process, carefully digesting each sentence as it comes. The out-and-out favourite of all, Sunday and week-day, is Wesley. There the volumes stand upon a shelf above the door—the "Notes," the "Sermons," the "Journals," and beside them two or three odd volumes of the "Christian Library." Jeremy Taylor's "Holy Living and Dying," is the most enriched with traces of soiled thumb and forefinger. There, too, is "Josephus," and Treffry's "Eternal Sonship," relieved by smaller volumes of Methodist biography.

They have passed away now, that old race of preachers, and a passionate devotion to their memory inspires thousands of the English-speaking race the wide world over. We recall them for a moment that we may render tribute to one phase of their work that is specially to be remembered in these days of demand for national education. Not so many years ago, in country towns and villages, the chief supply of books of every sort was through the preacher. The monthly book-parcel was quite an event. With saddle-bags well filled the preachers went their rounds, eagerly greeted in homes to which they brought the only reading. From this source it was that Dan'el obtained his select library, and his knowledge of many scores of books that he had never seen, but of which he had heard from the preacher.

Here, then, aproned, and in shirt sleeves, sits Brother Dan'el. A face that we can recall as easily as if we had but just left the shoemaker's shop,—as entirely original as his opinions. We see it still: that round bullet-head with its thick hair, which would not be smoothed down over his forehead, but stood persistently on end in an unruly and altogether un-Methodistical fashion; that forehead, straight and narrow, seamed and furrowed with deep wrinkles; the bristling eyebrows, and under them the broad-rimmed spectacles, covering on one side a green patch, (an accident in boyhood had hopelessly finished the work of that eye,) while on the other side peered the surviving partner, generally half over the broad silver rim,—a sharp quick busy eye, that looked as if it were perfectly aware that it had to do business for two, and meant to do it thoroughly; the short broad nose, "tip-tilted," perhaps, but by no means "like the petal of a flower;" the long upper lip, and then the little mouth pursed together as if it were always going to whistle, and lengthwise on each side ran the deep furrows draining into themselves the shallower rivulets and rills of wrinkles that crossed the face in every direction.

What a life of consistent devotion he lived! His religion was certainly theological; fiercely so sometimes, as even Fletcher could be in his polemics; a garrisoned city, full of defences and sharp definitions, of points and proofs. Yet it was as certainly the unswerving service of God, as that which was dearer than life; it was the hearty cleaving of his whole nature to the Redeemer, and a quiet joy in Him; as if within the buttressed walls there lay a garden of the Lord, well kept and dressed, wherein grew the Tree of Life, and where often "the voice of the Lord" was heard walking, in "the cool of the day."

What a world of quiet humour lay in him, and what a world of shrewd common-sense! Now and then there was perhaps a tinge of bitterness, a tone of sarcasm. Most folks readily forgave it, and as readily accounted for it. Betsey Quorm, his wife, was dead. She had never become more than plain Betsey Quorm; not good enough to be "sister," not respected enough to be "Mrs.," she had lived, and died, and was buried, as her tombstone testified, plain Betsey Quorm. And a thorn in the flesh she had been to Dan'el almost all the days of their wedded life. Perhaps that was the worst of it,— that she was *only a thorn in the flesh*,—that without doing or saying any great harm that one could take hold of, all she said and did somehow pricked, and fretted, and rankled, and festered, in a very unpleasant fashion. Only a thorn! Why, is there anything else that can compare with it? A man may be a very master of all sword-practice, a champion with the quarter-staff and the cudgel, but what are these against a *thorn?* The law redresses injury and wrong, but what legal skill can touch a thorn? A coat of mail may defy the tough lance that thrusteth sure, but what defence has a man against a thorn in the flesh? Little wonder that her influence lingered yet in a flavour of bitterness that betrayed itself at times, especially upon some topics.

"Wives," said Dan'el, "be like pilchards; when they be good they be only middlin'; but when they be bad, they *be* bad, sure 'nough."

II.

The Old Clock.

THE old clock stood in the corner of the cobbler's shop, and was, with but one exception, the most precious bit of furniture that he possessed.

The little shelf of books was very dear, but Wesley's works would have gone, "Notes," and "Sermons," and all, before the clock. Indeed there was only one thing that would have had any chance beside it. That was an old green-baize covered Bible, with loose leaves; dear, as the Book of precious promises from which every day Dan'el drew strength and peace and hope, it was dearer because on the fly leaf, amongst many family names and sundry accounts and entries, came the writing in a large straggling hand: "*My Mother's Bible. July,* 1832." Away in the quiet little churchyard was a grave, carefully tended, made beautiful with simple flowers; and at its head a stone that explained this date. Here rested John Quorm "of this parish," who died 1820. Here also slept Margery Quorm, wife of the above, who departed this life July 16th, 1832; and underneath this name was the text: "*I bowed down heavily, as one that mourneth for his mother.*" Little wonder that the Bible was dear.

But what could there be in a clock? It was an old-fashioned clock in a tall wooden case, that solemnly ticked in the corner,—slowly and solemnly ticked the minutes through, duly "giving warning" five minutes before the hour; striking deliberately, as if it stayed to count each stroke, and then settling down for another solemn hour's work. Yet solemn as it was, and much above all trifling, there was a strange little bit of humour on the very face of it. A round, chubby face with two round eyes was intended to represent the moon, and had been formerly connected with workings that marked the lunar changes and quarterings; but by some mishap it had slipped down, and one eye now peeped out of the corner with a cunning look, that seemed to say:

'You think me an old sober-sides who has not a

bit of fun in him, but that's all you know about it." And one almost expected to see a sly wink half shut that cunning little eye.

But these things,—its solemn ticking and its sly peeping,—however noteworthy they may have been, could not explain how it came to have such a place in Dan'el's heart of hearts. This was its story.

Daniel was about seventeen years of age when his father died. "Of course," said everybody, "of course old Mrs. Quorm will leave the place now. Pity but what young Dan'el was a few years older." Old Mrs. Quorm's relatives had actually gone to the length of making arrangements for her removal. But it had never crossed Dan'el's mind; and when he heard of it he simply stared with the one little sharp eye, and asked, "Whatever for?" and looked so amazed, and asked it with such angry surprise, that the relatives took a little longer time to think of it, in which time Daniel settled the matter in his own way.

He at once took upon his young shoulders all the care and toil of manhood. He never questioned how he should do, but just sat down in his father's place, and rose early and sat late, and worked away with a will that would have discovered the North-West Passage, much less sufficed to keep the old roof over the dear mother's head. It was a constant joy to him that she whom he loved so dearly, was so dependent on his thrift and industry. The very tools caught the impulse of such a generous motive. The hammer never rang so merrily in the old man's time; even the tough leather, and the hard lapstone might have had a heart in them somewhere, and never did their part so well—so all Penwinnin declared.

One night Dan'el sat, long after every other worker in the village was fast asleep, busying that one little eye that seemed never to tire. As he bored, and stitched, and hammered, his mind dwelt upon his father's death, and many thoughts began to stir that had often come and gone with no very visible result—thoughts of death and immortality, memories of words and events that had impressed him in his very childhood, and now woke up from their long slumber with strange force; how that *he*, too, must pass away, and *whither should he go?*

Suddenly the old clock in the corner took up the message with its slow and solemn ticking. In that still hour it kept repeating with measured beat, and strange monotony, its brief sentence—*For ever,—where?* FOR EVER,—WHERE? FOR EVER,—WHERE? Without a pause for a moment, without a break, it ticked on its dreadful question. Every other sound was hushed, and in the lonely stillness the ticking clock seemed to become almost unbearably loud. It was troublesome, and Daniel hammered more vigorously; but the ticking only grew louder; the question was pressed home only the more closely. Distinct and incessant it repeated itself, *For ever,—where? For ever,—where?* Daniel's deepest feelings began to be stirred. The memory of his father's last words broke upon him,—" Good-bye, Daniel, but not for ever." And again, slow and solemn, the old clock took up its strain,—" *For ever,—where? For ever,—where?*" Daniel could bear it no longer. He rose, laid down his work, and resolved to stop this persistent messenger. He walked over to it, and opened the narrow door. More loudly the question began, " For ever," but before it could be finished Daniel put his finger on the pendulum. At once all was still, and he returned to his work.

But the silence was more impressive than the slow ticking, and from within himself a voice began to say some plain things.

" Dan'el," it whispered, " thou art a coward and a fool." " So I am," he cried aloud, as he flung down his work, and as the tears gathered in his eyes. " Stopping the clock won't stop the time. The moments are going all the same, whether I hear them or not. And am I going with them, *for ever,— where? for ever,—where?* No; I'll set it agoing again, for it does no good to stop it."

Bravely he set it off once more. But the work

lay at his feet, and with clasped hands and head hung down, he gave himself up to thoughts that impressed him so deeply: the thought of God, of His claims, of His goodness, of His righteousness, grew upon him; of sin, of its horribleness and its awful peril. All the sins of his life began to rise up before him, especially the one great sin of neglecting and forgetting God; and amidst it all came every now and then that slow, solemn ticking: *For ever,—where? For ever,—where?* His distress became unbearable. He flung himself upon his knees, and cried, "O God, be merciful to me a sinner!" Long he wrestled in earnest prayer; but all was in vain. No help, no light, no peace came. In despair he ceased to pray, and buried his face in his hands. "*For ever,—where? For ever,—where?*" rang again from the clock, in that lonely silence.

What could he do? Goaded and driven on by that dreadful message, whither could he fly? All he could do was to fall, as a poor helpless sinner, into the Saviour's arms. The tears fell faster as he flung himself helplessly on the stool, and groaned: "Oh Lord, a broken heart Thou wilt not despise! Look at mine. Broken and crushed, have mercy upon me, and save me." That moment light dawned upon him. He rested upon Christ, his crucified Redeemer, *and that was everything.* Helpless and undone, he just simply clung to the Cross of Christ, and there he found what the thousands of the redeemed have found there,—pardon, and peace, and heaven. For his sins the Lord had died; for him that Life had been laid down. The clear light of the Holy Spirit, who is come to testify of Jesus, lit up all the purpose of the Cross, and revealed all the mercy of God in Christ. Daniel knelt, hushed in adoring gratitude. Again through the stillness came that message from the corner, welcomed now with strangely different feelings—*For ever,—where? For ever,—where?* From Daniel's heart there burst the rapturous response: "Glory be to Thee, O Lord! with Thee for ever! 'He that believeth hath everlasting life!'"

As he rose from his knees the old clock struck twelve. "The 'old things are passed away,'" he whispered, "and 'all things are become new.'" Well may the old clock strike twelve, and finish this strange night; ay, and that old life! A new day begins for me." And he left it in the darkness ticking on its solemn message: *For ever,—where? For ever,—where?*

Reader,—hast thou heard the message? What is the answer? Onward, downward, towards the eternal darkness? or forward, upward, towards the sunny distance of the everlasting light?

III.

"My Mother's Bible."

DEAR old Dan'el would never forgive me, I am sure, if he knew that I told the story of the clock, and passed over that which was treasured more sacredly, and came somehow to be always mixed up with the clock,— *his Mother's Bible.*

An old-fashioned book, in a faded green-baize cover which could scarcely manage to hold the looser leaves that projected beyond the dark brown edges,—it was certainly nothing to look at. A second-hand bookseller would probably have grudged anything more than its worth as waste paper. But gilt edges and gold clasp, morocco binding, the designs of Doré, or the wild grandeur of Martin's fancies, could never have made any book so dear as was that old Bible to Dan'el Quorm.

Nor was the inside of the book more promising in appearance. You opened it, and under the black threads that held the baize together were sundry papers—Methodist quarterly Class-tickets, mostly bearing the name of Margery Quorm; old receipts and prescriptions in faded brown ink and queer spelling,—"For takin' down proud flesche." "How to kep henseggs;" or brief headings with a long list of remedies for "Crick in the backe," and sundry ailments. One of the most curious entries was the "*Charm for a seal.*" *

In the same faded ink were bills and accounts scrawled upon the cover and extending to the blank leaf, even intruding upon the title-page and the dedication, so that the most high and mighty Prince James was obscured under "perchas of lether," and memoranda about the rent. To Dan'el's mind these entries were like "tables of the money-changers,

---

* Which ran thus :—"To be said three times :

'There was three Angels come from the west—
The wan brot fiar, and the other brot frost,
And the other brot the book of Jesu Christ.
In the Name of the Father, and of the Son, and
of the Holy Ghost.'"

and seats of them that sold doves,"—defiling the holy place; intruders that he would fain have driven forth from the sanctuary, but that unfortunately they were fixtures, and could not be removed without damaging the Holy Temple itself.

There was one more entry. Across the faded receipts, in bold and large letters, came a more recent writing which stood like an inscription over the temple porch, explaining all its sanctity and preciousness—*My Mother's Bible.*

Who could tell all that this book was to Dan'el Quorm? It was verily more precious than gold, yea, than fine gold.

Never was the laboured missal of the monk so beautifully illuminated as was this old worn Bible to Dan'el. Every incident of it was illustrated to him, and every page was bordered with memories that brightened and enriched it with more than crimson and gold.

Back in the dim age of his childhood, in the earliest memory of his life, there was this treasured volume. It was the memory that stood like the frontispiece of his life. He saw himself as a little lad beside his mother's knee, looking up with loving wonder into that gentle face: she a picture of purity and sweetness in her Methodist dress and the simple white cap that gathered around a face not beautiful, but more than beautiful, just an embodiment of sweetness and light, in which lurked no possibility of distrust, or fear, or grumbling; every feature telling of a love such as could hope all things, and believe all things,—yet no weakness, but that combination of gentleness and strength which constitutes the love that can endure all things. The neat white muslin kerchief folded under the black dress completed the portrait.

Here the little lad kneeled to learn his first lessons, and the associations of those early days, however illogical and foolish they may have been, were the most influential and imperishable of his life. Dan'el Quorm, an old fellow as tough and unsentimental as his own shoe leather, as sharp and shrewd as his shining awl or his keen knife, could not for the life of him come to believe any otherwise than that the sweet face and gentle voice and loving manner, that the very dress and bearing, came somehow from the teachings of his Mother's Bible.

Memories of her were wrapt up with its most familiar portions. Dan'el could never hear the story of faithful Noah, of the good lad Joseph, of little Moses, of Joshua and Gideon, of David and Daniel, and the more familiar incidents in the life of Jesus, but they became pictures which her sweet voice explained and impressed.

Nor was it only in childhood that such vivid

memories had illustrated the work. As you turned over the pages you came to marks enclosing many of the passages; lines drawn around some verses, and having a date written on the margin. To a stranger just four ink marks about some words: to Dan'el they were the chronicles of his history; they marked the most memorable incidents of his life.

From the beginning to the end of the forty-sixth Psalm were these distinguishing marks, elevating it into a kind of monument, the Ebenezer stone of a grateful memory. And this was the event that it recorded. Dan'el was yet a little lad when the French wars had drained the country of money and of labour. In common with thousands of others, the little family of Penwinnin was sorely pinched by it. But want was not the only, not even the worst trouble. Everybody believed that Napoleon was about to land somewhere on the Cornish Coast. There where the sea locked them in on three sides, West, North, and South of them, they could see the ocean, the highway of their enemies—in times, too, when newspapers were very few, and seldom reached that far-off corner, and when amongst the excited people rumours were rife and always terrible and threatening—there was enough to make folks uneasy. More than once a messenger had hurried to the village with the tidings that the French were coming—by this time had landed; some fisherman or smuggler had seen them at dawn, and came in with the news. The frightened people prepared to save themselves as best they could; some would fly eastward; others would escape to the rocky summits and crags of the hills. One stalwart mother in Israel grasped a pitchfork, and went through the village street rousing the people to arm themselves with whatever weapons they could find, and to follow her, and they would keep out " Mounseer." At such times Dan'el had been taken by a gentle hand and led into his mother's room: there, kneeling by her side, he had watched with wonder that calm faith renew itself, as she read the words: *" God is our Refuge and Strength, a very present Help in trouble. Therefore will not we fear, though the earth be removed, and though the mountains be carried into the midst of the sea. . . . The Lord of Hosts is with us; the God of Jacob is our Refuge."* Then there followed the prayer, in which his mother poured out her trustful heart before the Lord. And little Dan'el came down the stairs at her side, with such a contempt for Napoleon and all the Frenchmen, and such a sense of safety, as if the overshadowing wings of the most High verily enfolded them.

Another illustration was in the book of Isaiah. Here, too, the ordinary reader could but find a text enclosed in lines, and beside them the entry of a date. But to Dan'el there was a picture of a darkened room, where in the dim light knelt that mother and a lad of seventeen, he fatherless, and she a widow. They knelt in silence for awhile; then the pages of the Bible had been opened and the sweet voice read with calm firmness the words, *"Fear not, ... for thy Maker is thine husband; the Lord of Hosts is His name; and thy Redeemer the Holy one of Israel."* And again they knelt in silence—a silence in which those tones and words sank down into the lad's heart, making her in her sorrow and loneliness sacredly dear to him; and filling him with the strength and purpose that henceforth he so lovingly rendered.

There were other illustrations. But we must linger only over one more. One more distinctly marked, a scene more vivid and powerful to Dan'el's mind than any other. Not much to look at was there in that text with the lines around it and with the date written in the corner.

> Arise, let us go hence.
> July 16th, 1832.

But Dan'el saw in it a picture that could never fade or grow dim. He saw himself seated beside the bed with the Bible before him. He was looking with tears upon her whom he felt he could not look upon much longer. That faint failing breath too plainly told the story. The face, though pinched with suffering, was still beautiful in its placid calm and fulness of love. Since noon a wild thunderstorm had crashed and rolled about the hills, but now as the sun went down the clouds had cleared, and in the cool fresh evening the fragrance of sweet flowers and the singing of the birds and the radiant sunset glow came together through the opened window and filled the little room.

"Read to me, dear," she whispered faintly. And her son, loath to turn his eyes from her face, at once opened at the favourite chapter, the fourteenth of St. John. Slowly he repeated the verses, only now and then looking at the book. As the sun sank lower the rays slowly crept round the room, and now they were shining upon the bed.

"*Whither I go ye know, and the way ye know. . . . . Let not your heart be troubled, neither let it be afraid.*"

The light crept on until it touched the pillow, and just caught the withered helpless hand and the frilled sleeve.

Dan'el read on, "*These things have I spoken unto you, being yet present with you. But the Comforter, which is the Holy Ghost, whom the Father will send in My Name, He shall teach you all things, and bring all things to your remembrance, whatsoever I have said unto you.*"

The light crept onward until it rested upon the border of the white cap, and almost touched the soft white hair.

"Peace I leave with you," Dan'el continued; "My peace I give unto you." The feeble lips whispered the words as they were read. "Let not your heart be troubled, neither let it be afraid."

The light crept further until now it fell upon all the face. It seemed to touch the cheeks with the ruddy glow of youth, and lit up every feature with a rare beauty.

"Arise, let us go hence," whispered Dan'el with faltering voice. But no whispered response came from those half-open lips. The hand dropped helplessly towards Dan'el, and as it was caught and passionately kissed, she passed away.

He kneeled there in his great burst of sorrow, while the light faded; the long twilight sank into darkness, and when Dan'el looked up again he could not see her.

"Let me see her no more," he muttered as he rose and turned, feeling for the door. "She has arisen and has gone hence. 'They need no candle, neither light of the sun; for the Lord God giveth them light: and they shall reign for ever and ever,'" . . . .

*   *   *   *   *

There were other texts thus made to chronicle the principal incidents; one or two that Dan'el might have been less willing to explain. But as notable events in his life, and as a faithful historian of them they were duly recorded in his Mother's Bible.

One was dated in August of the next year, when things at home had come to be in much need of a gentle hand and of a woman's care. Together with much amused talk amongst the neighbours in which Dan'el's name was first associated with that of Betsey Crocker, there appeared four emphatic lines around the verse, "*It is not good that the man should be alone.*"

"Betsey knew what she was a-doin' of!" was the uncharitable opinion of the village gossips. An opinion that had very little other ground for its uncharitableness than this, that Betsey happened to be twelve years older than her beau. Within six months of the wedding came another entry. Suffice it to say that it completed this portion of his history: lines were drawn about the passage: "*Art thou loosed from a wife? seek not a wife.*"

Perhaps the fault was not *altogether* on his wife's side. Dan'el had an ideal of womanhood so lofty and pure, that very few could have attained to it, and poor blundering Betsey was always measured by the vivid memory of what his mother had been.

IV.

Brother Quorm's Prejudice.

ABOVE everything else my friend Dan'el was a Class-leader. He was good at making shoes or mending them; good at doing the bit of garden in front of his place; good at an argument, and many a man dropped into the shoemaker's for a talk; good at a sermon, as appeared from his appointments on that huge Circuit-plan. But it was as a Class-leader that you had Dan'el at his best.

His two Classes had more than sixty members, a fair half of that flourishing Society at Penwinnin.

Here it was, at these Classes, that Dan'el came

out strong. Pithy, plain, common-sensed, with a depth of pity and tenderness in his soul, here perhaps Dan'el was at his best. So wise, so simple, so practical.

But here, too, it was that Dan'el's prejudice betrayed itself. There were moments when he would come out in a sharp, hasty way, and run full tilt against some notion that he sought to demolish. Dan'el was a man to whom nothing was so intolerably offensive as a *proverb*. All that a pun was to Doctor Johnson, and worse, a proverb was to him. "The embodiment of a nation's wisdom," "the simplest expression of life's philosophy," "the most compact summing-up of universal experience," as others called them, to Dan'el they were the grossest delusions—"half truths and all lies."

And making some allowance for Daniel's prejudice, it must be owned that not many things are more provoking to an earnest man than to find one's careful arguments evaded or overthrown by some pet proverb, "like as if 'twas the Gospel itself" as he used to say; or when a point is clearly established by some irresistible instance, to find it all coolly pooh-poohed by the ready saying that, "it's only the exception that proves the rule." If anything might vex an argumentative and logical saint Dan'el thought that this was of all things the most likely to produce such a result.

"They that made 'em had enough mother-wit for to see and know what they do mean," he would explain to sympathizing listeners, "but as for most o' them there that use 'em, they have'n't got sense enough for to see when they be true and when they be lies."

Yet even such inconveniences as these Dan'el could have endured. The evil became unbearable when it assumed a religious form. The habitual phrases in which people contentedly excused themselves, and under which they took shelter from every duty, these most provoked his ire.

Old Farmer Gribble, who lived in the village, was a ready example of Dan'el's point.

"There's Muster Gribble in to the farm in here,— just like a snail drags hisself back, horns an' all, into his shell; or, like to a dew-worm that hears you a comin' an' starts back into his hole in a minute, that be just how he'll hide up in a proverb. I said to him the other day, 'Farmer, you've had a capital harvest. I want you to give me something for our Missions.'

"'Missions!' he cries out, 'Missions! No, Dan'el, I hold with Paul, that charity begins at home.' Then when I tell him that Paul knew better than to write such nonsense, and that there's no such thing in the Bible, says he, in his drawlin' way:—

"'Well, if it ben't there, Dan'el, *it ought to be there, for I've a heard it a'most so often!*'

"That's the way with lots of 'em. There's poor Bob Byles, the drunken backslider, keeps sayin' what wonderful comfort he finds in that there passage, '*'Tis a long lane that han't got no turnin'*;' like as if it were a sure promise that he'll come right some day."

Now and then people ventured to speak in defence of such sayings, and of the good they did,—as when the man who was tempted to stay from the Class-meeting through the rough weather, thought of the words, "Faint heart never won fair lady," and broke through the snare.

Dan'el would look up at you with his one little eye, and nod his rough head: "Why there never was a bad thing yet that didn't do some good. The Devil hisself have sometimes worritted me into prayin' and watchin'. There, look 'pon that there," he said one day, when arguing the matter thus, and pointed through the window to a dilapidated rook that was tied to a stick, and swung in the breeze of the April day, scaring his comrades from the young green wheat. "That old fellow sometimes eat grubs and insects, but Farmer Gribble shot him for eatin' his corn. They do some good; but it's to stop their doin' harm that I should like to hang 'em up. Tinker Tim, who went to prison the other day, was a rare good hand at grindin' of razors and knives, but he was sent across the seas for settin' corn stacks a-fire. Why there wouldn't be any harm in the world if it weren't done by things that be some good."

How Dan'el met many of these sayings we need not stay to tell; but how he dealt with the proverbial phrases of the Class-meetings and of religious talk, is worthy of being recorded. Words with him were ammunition—flung out in a sharp, jerky style, like an irregular fire of musketry. Now they were grape shot, stinging and effective; now bullets, sharp and silencing; now cannon balls, sweeping with thunder; now shells bursting into atoms fine fancies, and the tall talk of some real or imaginary opponent. An artillery used with most manifest pleasure to demolish these refuges of idle and mendicant souls. For words to be abused in proverbs thus was to Dan'el much as it had been to some sturdy old puritan had he seen honest bullets beaten into roofing for the shelter of traitors and rebels. Never did the one little eye twinkle with such flashes of indignation and joyous humour, or the pursed-up mouth so fling out its words, as when he demolished such religious phrases,—good in themselves, but made false and harmful by those who used them.

V.

Brother Quorm at Class.

BROTHER Quorm had two Classes; and, as we have said, had altogether on his books more than half the Society at Penwinnin.

The larger and more popular Class met at eight o'clock on the Sunday morning. They met in what was called by courtesy, 'the PARLOUR'—really the sanded front-kitchen —at Thomas Toms'. Next to the leader's own name, was that of Sally Toms, or " Granny," as everybody called her, who had her bed in that room, and always lay there. An old woman bordering upon a hundred, she had been in the Society for eighty years, and declared that she should "take her death" if she "did'n go to mittin' regular,"—which was scarcely accurate, as the meeting always came to her. There she lay, with the thin withered fingers clasped on the clean white sheet; the face, with its clear ruddy complexion, bordered by the hair of such bleached softness, and framed by the cap that gathered round and set it off like a picture. Cut off as she was from all other services, this united singing and prayer, the faces of her old friends, and the talk about "good things," was her solace and strength. There was no doubt about it: it did her good, as she said, "Body and soul, bless the Lord!—body and soul." And to those who came, it was as good as a sermon—better than some sermons perhaps—to look at her.

Altogether it was an arrangement to meet the case of an old member, such as might well be imitated in thousands of places; an arrangement too by which the Church secured those holy influences and ripe utterances which she can least afford to lose. If the mountain can't come to Mahomet, there is just one other expedient—let Mahomet go to the mountain. Take the Class-meeting to the old sick members; if not always, at least once or twice in the quarter. This is better than having the names run on page after page, till some day dropped as unknown by a new leader—

cutting off from membership some of the saintliest heirs of glory. There was much grace, and much wisdom, and much gain every way, in that kindly little arrangement.

And how cosy and snug the place used to feel! A vestry has not any *homeliness* in it, somehow. You feel that folks don't live there, and you can't readily make yourself quite "at home" in it. There, at Thomas Toms,' was the canary hanging in the window, that always began to sing when the hymn was given out, just as if he had been a regular member of the Class. But he was summarily expelled from Society by having an anti-macassar flung over the cage; an indignity against which he mildly protested by the utterance of an occasional mournful note. There, over the mantel-piece, were the shining brasses and pans; and on the walls figured the quaint old over-coloured drawings of the Noah's Ark, and other scriptural subjects. And at the week-day Class were homelier touches that made men talk about religion in a simple, every-day tone, the like of which it is hard to get in a vestry. Why there was the pan of bread set down before the fire to "plumb;" or the savoury baking of "the pasties" proclaimed itself delicately from the oven; and on the hearth-rug lay a pair of little shoes and socks. Much of that strong social union to which Methodism has been so greatly indebted, and which in old time she so carefully fostered, came from the fact that the people went from "house to house;" the Class-meetings and the prayer-meetings were in the houses of the people, and the Church itself was not unfrequently a "Church in the house."

You could not have been long in Brother Dan'el's Class, without seeing how much they all owed to the presence of old "Granny" Toms. There she lay like a beautiful picture of the faith that could comfort and guide and sustain them; a voice on before bidding them fear not, and a radiant face turning as if to let them know what light, and peace, and joy were on there.

Dan'el used perpetually to clench his argument and point his moral by reference to Granny. When young members began to talk of their fears and of hindrances, how the one sharp little eye would look towards the old saint, uttering a dozen notes of exclamation all at once.

"Hindrances!!! Hindrances!! Aw, my dear! Begin to talk about hindrances, and mother here 'll tell a story about hindrances. Granny can mind hearin' 'em ring the Church bells 'cause they'd clean drove the Methodists out o' the parish."

Granny would have confirmed it with words, but that Dan'el knew her habit of entering with much minuteness into the pedigree and circumstances of everybody concerned—so he only waited for her

D

preliminary nod, and then hurried on again before she had time to begin.

"Hindrances, my dear! Why she can mind hearin' 'em talk of how a man down to Penzance was put to prison for blasphemy 'cause he said the Lord had forgiven his sins. Why, my dear, doan't let us go talkin' about it—we be goin' to heaven in silver slippers. Why, mother, you used to walk sixteen miles 'pon the Sunday."

"Rain or fine," said Granny with a nod.

"Iss, we be goin' in silver slippers," and then as a merry twinkle played about that sharp little eye, and it rested a moment upon the smart ribbons or flowered bonnet—"In *silver slippers!*—and that be the hindrance. We do make our own hindrances. It be easier to go barefoot than in tight shoes. And silver slippers is poor things for any journey, but most of all for going to the Celestial City. No wonder that we go limpin', and talk about making little progress and about our hindrances. Folks with tight shoes 'll get corns,—and serve 'em right too,—and then every road is hard to travel, and every bit of a rise is a mountain. Rain now-a-days is a hindrance; but in mother's time it wasn't. For in the old times the big bonnets and long cloaks were like umbrella and everything else, and 'cats an' dogs' weren't a hindrance then. But now we go wearin such fine feathers an' things, that a sprinkle of rain an' they're spoiled. And I wish they were all that was spoiled, for it wouldn't be any great matter if a good deal of 'em was washed away. But it spoils the temper, and it vexes and worrits all the grace out o' folks; and then ever so much time goes in trying to get it right again. Talk about temptations an' hindrances! Why I don't see how it can be much other. The old enemy goes drivin' about like Jehu in his chariot, and he can see us in a minute with all this finery, and he comes poisonin' such folks with pride an' conceit. He's sent many, I'll warrant to the dogs, like Jezebel, all through their tired heads and furbelows, who'd have been all right if they had just gone along plain and simple. O' course anybody can put as much pride into old mother's cap here as into anything else. Seemin' to me 'tis best to go in what other folks 'll take least notice of either way; for then we shan't think much of ourselves, an' slippin' along in the crowd the enemy isn't so likely to single us out. I've seen it advertised very often in the papers—'tourists' suits.' Well, they may be very good; but for our journey I don't believe there's anything that's so good, or so comfortable as what I've read of somewhere else—'tis' homespun, and you can't buy it anywhere, so we must all learn to make it—*Be clothed with humility.* A hindrance it is, sure 'nough, in a good many ways. Folks be kept so long a-'tidivatin' o' theirselves that they're sure to get to meetin' ten minutes late; an' that's all the worse because they take so long a-gettin' ready that they're sure not to have a minute for a bit o' prayer afore they start. I've heard tell about a man who preached from them words— '*There appeared a great wonder in Heaven—a woman.*' But he ought to ha' gone on an' finished it—'*a woman clothed with the sun and upon her head a crown of twelve stars.*' Now seemin' to me the wonder was that anybody dressed so shinin' an' glitterin' ever got to Heaven, and it will be a wonder if some folks manage to get there with their heads all covered over with feathers an' flowers an' all the rest of it.

"No, we hardly know what hindrances be now-a-days, and tho few there are don't come from heaven above, or earth beneath; but they come out of our own pride and folly, or out of our neglect. They, too, are *home-made*, every one of 'em, *home-made.*"

VI.

Brother Dan'el on "Slow and Sure."

THERE inside the door of Thomas Toms' parlour sat Jim Tregoning— a well-meaning kind of a man, whom people spoke of as "poor fellow;" and said how unfortunate he was. He had tried everything, from driving a van to selling patent medicines and hawking books. There he sat with an unmeaning smile upon his face, and large eyes looking on one place all through the hour, but never seeming to see anything. He was perpetually folding his red cotton handkerchief into a large pad, with which he stroked his hair down over his forehead, and then began to remake the pad. When his turn came he spoke with a sigh.

"How was he gettin' on? Well, he feared he was only a slow traveller heavenward. But there—he had many troubles and trials—fightin's without and fears within—and he hoped that his motter was *slow an' sure, slow an' sure;* for the race wasn't to the wise nor yet to the strong, but it were to the sure. If he could'nt fly he must walk, and if he couldn't walk he must creep; and if he wasn't so fast a traveller as some folks, he hoped he were just as sure."

The little eye twinkled—and yet there was a tone of pain and grief in the reply.

"La, Jim, whatever do 'e mean! 'Slow and sure, slow and sure.' Always the same. Never no forwarder, never no backwarder, but always a stickin' in the same place. I'll tell 'e what Jim. You 'slow and sure' folks be just like a faggot o' green furze 'pon the fire. You don't blaze nor burn; you do nothing but only steam, and fizz, and go fillin' the house with smeach and smoke. Do 'e get out o' this here way. *Strive* to enter in at the strait gate; but goin' along so slow you'll be sure not to get through un. Slow an' sure! Iss, sure to be too late! 'Tis what the folks said when they was a comin' to the Ark; but the floods came quick and sure 'pon them before they got to the Ark, and slow an' sure was drowned. Serve him right, too. The virgins was slow and sure when they were a-gone to buy oil for their lamps, and when they come back *the door was shut.* Slow an' sure! 'Tis damp powder that do burn like that there, Jim,—it'll choke 'e all with smoke, but it won't ever heave a rock in two, or do anybody a morsel o' good.

"I've heard em' say that horses that be stumblers be a'most sure to come down if you let 'em go along with a creepin' kind of a jog-trot. And that's how Christian folks fall in general; going along so slow an' sleepy, down they come all of a heap, knockin' theirselves all to bits a'most before they know where they are.

"An' then troubles an' trials—of course you do have them—heaps of 'em. What else can anybody expect? Slow and sure! Why, 'tis 'xactly like when I be walkin' to Redburn on a fair-day, and every van and cart and lumberin' waggon, and donkeys, and all the riff-raff and sharpers—they do all overtake me. But when you get in the train you go whizzing over their heads, and leave 'em behind, every one of 'em.

"Go creepin' along! Why o' course there's never a trouble or trial but it comes up to you. Spread your wings, Jim, spread your wings out, and fly! '*They that wait upon the Lord shall renew 'their strength;*' and shall mount—mount, Jim;— '*they shall mount up with wings as eagles.*' Old care is a black-winged, croaking old raven; but his croakin' can't get up so high as the eagle, it's down, down ever so far below; down under the clouds; and the eagle is up above 'em all, in the floods o' sunshine. '*They shall mount up with wings as eagles; they shall run, and not be weary; they shall walk, and not faint.*'

" My dear Jim, there ben't no such thing as this slow and sure o' yours. When the top do spin slow he's sure to come down. 'Tisn't the way the angels told Lot. *Escape for thy life; tarry not in all the plain;* and I don't think we shall get off easier than he did. And, 'tisn't the way Paul knew anything about; for says he, *Run the race set before you.* He don't say anything about creepin', and it be best to stick to the Word, Jim.

"'Slow an' sure'!—seem to me that everything be the other way about. The old Tempter, whatever other failin's he've got, ha'nt got that there— he do go about like a great roarin' lion, seeking whom he may devour, an' if we go creepin' along he's sure to come springin' out 'pon us all unawares —an' serve us right for we tempt 'en even if he could have had enough afore we come by. Time is swift and sure, Jim; and death is swift and sure. And then the love of Jesus is swift and sure. Ah! bless the Lord, how swift and sure that is you know, Jim, as well as the rest! ' *When* he was yet a great way off, his father saw him, and had compassion, and ran,—ran."—And Dan'el's voice spoke with a tenderness that brought the tears to every eye.—"No creepin' then, or walkin' either. He 'ran, and fell on his neck, and kissed him.' Ah, bless the Lord; that's His way always—and His way be always best!" And he brushed away the tears as he finished—"Come friends, let us sing a hymn,—

'My soul through my Redeemer's care,
 Saved from the second death I feel,
My eyes from tears of dark despair,
 My feet from falling into hell.

"Second verse,—

'Wherefore to Him my feet shall run;'

"That's it,—*run*.

'My eyes on His perfections gaze·
My soul shall live for God alone;
 And all within me shout His praise.'"

VII.

"It's the Lord's Will, you know."

IT was at the Class-meeting on the Tuesday night. The wild west wind came sweeping round the house fierce and furious—now rattling at the window, and roaring in the chimney, then sinking into a low moan, whining at the keyhole as if its blustering had failed, and it had taken to entreaty instead; then suddenly it grew enraged again, as if ashamed of its weakness, and seemed to make the very ground tremble as it roared and thundered away up the wild hill-side.

Here in the sanded front-room at Thomas Toms',

sat the members of Brother Quorm's Class. Only a few to-night, for many lived across the moors, and some a mile away over the fields; and even Dan'el could excuse those who tarried at home on such a night as this. The storm itself had nothing to do with the talk of that evening, only it came somehow to be inseparably bound up with the memories of it.

The meeting had opened quietly enough with a "trumpet metre," followed by a hearty prayer. Two or three had spoken, but it was not until Widow Pascoe's turn came that the memorable talk of that evening began. There she sat, in a huge bonnet of rusty black, the very capacious widow's cap gathered about a face which was always "in mourning." That mouth of itself rendered crape altogether superfluous,—the long thin lips drawn down at the corners, and tucked away under the wrinkles and furrows, as if to keep it in its place. The languidly-closed eyes, the solemn shake of the head, the deep sigh, and then the long-drawn melancholy words in which she told of her troubles and trials, were unfailing characteristics of her experience; and to-night her favourite phrases kept coming in continually—"submit to His will," "done and suffered His will." No belief was ever more deeply wrought into any heart than this into the widow's— that it was the will of the Heavenly Father that she should be always in trouble; to-day was given only that she might find in it some new sorrow; each hour came only to lay another burden upon her, and to-morrow already hinted at some threatening evil. She would almost have doubted her religion if she could not find in everything something to sigh over. With her the truest sign of grace was "to walk mournfully." Heaven itself to her mind was a sort of compensation paid to those who endured the hurts and damages of religion in this life.

As the widow finished, Dan'el looked up at her almost fiercely with his one little eye. But immediately a sad expression crept over it. "'Submit to His will,' 'Suffer His will.' Is that all that the will of God is for, that we may endure it, and suffer it!" And Dan'el sighed a great pitiful sigh. After a long pause, in which the wild storm outside seemed to burst with more fury, he went on in a gentler tone: "Bless His holy Name, He is our loving Father; and we go asking for grace to *submit* to His will, and go talking about suffering His will!"

Dan'el suddenly broke off his remarks, as if he had no hope of ever setting the widow right; and, with another pitiful sigh, he passed on to the next.

Now it happened that the next was John Trundle, the busy village shopkeeper. A man with whom business was the great end of life, and religion a very advisable precaution, in case of emergency; much as a man thinks it prudent to insure his life. Indeed religion was to him just that—a Prudential Assurance; and the Class-meeting was only the agency through which he paid his insurance money, a quarterly account. His little fortune had been invested in some adjoining Wheal Gambler,—a mine in which he was to find prodigious wealth; but the golden visions slowly faded, and the mine was given up, having afforded only a deep, dark grave in which Mr. Trundle had buried most of his savings. Vexation and disappointment had brought him more regularly to Class; at least for a little while. Perhaps it was the moaning wind outside, or perhaps it was Sister Pascoe's mournfulness, or perhaps, and probably, it was the prevailing thought of his mind, that led him at once to allude to his recent losses. He had been going through deep waters, he said, had been called to pass through severe trials; "but there," said he, "it be the Lord's will, you know," and he hoped he should have the grace to bear it.

Before John Trundle had finished, it was evident that something was moving Dan'el's soul to its depths. The little eye opened with astonishment; the mouth was pursed up as if it were going to whistle with amazement, the round bullet head nodded sharply, and at last the words were jerked out somewhat fiercely.

"Umph! 'The Lord's will, you know!' Well, I must say I don't know it, John, and I don't think it, either. Not a bit of it. The Lord's will! I went over the moors t'other night, without a lantern, and tumbled in a big hole, and I said, 'Dan'el, you are an old stoopid for to go wi'out your lantern. *serve you right.*' But I didn't think it was the Lord's will, John, and I hope I shouldn't be so foolish again."

Then he stopped suddenly as if a new idea had shot across his mind, and passing over the next two or three he turned to an old man who sat in the corner of the room by the fire.

It was dear old Frankey Vivian. There he sat in the ruddy glow of the firelight, with the deep shadows of the corner behind him. Very feeble, weakness had given him an appearance of age much beyond his years; and as he leaned there upon his stick in this light, he looked like some old patriarch who had turned his back upon the shadows of the world, and was standing on the threshold of the celestial city, waiting only for the summons to come in. His case was too common in those mining districts before the recent improvements had been introduced. Climbing up the ladders by which men came from immense depths below; coming from the hot air underground in wet clothes, and stepping at once into the keen winds that swept "up to grass," as the surface was called—poetically, for scarce a blade was to be found in all the stony waste of the mine;—these things had done their work upon a naturally weak constitution, and now he was in the last stage of asthmatic consumption. Unable to work, and having a large family to be cared for somehow, his was a sad story. He lived so near by that he could easily slip in " to the meetin'," and very rarely was his corner vacant even on such a night as this.

With a touch of tenderness, and with a very evident relief, Dan'el turned to him.

"The Lord bless thee, dear Frankey. Come, tell us what the Lord's will is to thee."

The pale, wasted face moved with deep feeling; the thin white hands passed to and fro over the handle of the stick nervously; the tears gathered in his eyes:

" The Lord's will!" gasped the old man. "Why this, my dear leader, this—'Goodness and mercy shall follow me all the days o' my life; and I will dwell in the house o' the Lord for ever!' Bless His holy Name—that, nothing else but that. Why there was only last Saturday afternoon: I was very poorly; my cough shook me all to bits, and I was lying 'pon my bed. Yet my soul was full o' praise to God for all His goodness. Bless His Name, I says, why this here shakin' cough be only like the joltin' o' the van over the ruts and stones as it be a carryin' us home. And some day it'll give the last jolt and stop right afore the door o' my Father's house, and, bless Him, He'll come out to take His child into His arms, and I shall be home for ever and ever. To think of it! *home!* ay, and with breath for to praise my Lord too. I was a sayin' over them words, 'Bless the Lord, ye His angels, that excel in strength.' *Excel in strength.* And I thought how I would be a-flyin' in a little while, and how I would sweep the harp, and how swift I would go for my dear Lord, a sailin' along 'pon a pair o' glorious wings, how grand it would be! My soul was all full of it, when up come my wife, and she sat down at the foot o' the bed, and she flings her hands all helpless like down before her.

"'Frankey,' says she, a'most a chokin,' 'Frankey, whatever shall us do. There ben't a bit o' bread in the house agen the children come home.'

"'What shall us do, my dear?' I says. 'Why think of the Blessed Father Who tells us to call upon Him in the day of trouble, and He will hear us. And He will too, I know.'

"'Seemin' to me He must have forgot us,' says she, bursting out a-cryin'.

"'Forgot us, wife!' I says. 'Forgot us! Bless His holy Name, it *wouldn't be like Him.* He don't ever forget. He has been round and about us, our Friend and Helper these twenty years, and it wouldn't be like Him to leave us now, just when we want Him most. That isn't the way He does.' And I began to say over the hundred and forty-sixth Psalm that I do dearly love. 'While I live I will praise the Lord: I will sing praises unto my God while I have any being. . . . Happy is he that hath the God of Jacob for his help, whose hope is in the Lord his God. There, wifie, isn't that pretty music now. Which keepeth truth for ever. Hear that,' I says. 'Keepeth truth for ever. Which giveth food to the hungry. Bless Him, why it's put there a-purpose for you and me.'

"'Well,' says she, wipin' her eyes with her apron, 'I s'pose it be the Lord's will, and we must bear it.'

"The tears came in my eyes then. 'O, my dear! Don't 'e talk like that,' I says, 'don't 'e talk like that there, now. It be no more the will of our blessed Father that our children should want bread than it be your will or mine. It do hurt me to hear folks talk like that about my Lord. *It is not the will of your Father which is in heaven, that one of these little ones should perish*, that be the Lord's will,' I says. '*Like as a Father pitieth his children, so the Lord pitieth them that fear Him*. Why, the Book is full of it, and we ought not to go talkin' about our Blessed Father like that.'

"Well, just then there came a double knock to the door. It ben't very often that we do have a letter, so the wife jumps up and runs down stairs. In a minute she shouts up to me,

"'Frankey, here's a letter from our boy in Australia.' And then in a minute more she comes runnin' up to me, and cries out—'Why, there's a five-pound note in it. Bless his dear heart!' And tears of joy ran down our cheeks.

"Ah, wifie," says I, holdin' up the note, "look here; *that* be the Lord's will, and we must bear it. Bless His holy Name, He '*keepeth truth for ever.*'"

Every eye was dimmed as Frankey finished his simple story. Dan'el now had a fair field, and all the gathering feelings and thoughts of the evening broke out with a triumph.

"That's it, Frankey," he cried. "Sure enough that's just it. The Lord's will isn't starving children. '*Which executeth judgment for the oppressed; which giveth food to the hungry.* '*The Lord's will, you know.*' Why people don't stop to think what they mean when they talk about it. The words, perhaps, are right enough by theirselves, but folks use 'em to wrap up more nonsense and more sin than any other five words in the world. There's poor Jem Polsue, lives up to Bray. I dropt in to see him a few days a-gone.

He lost his wife of fever; and he himself wasn't expected to get over it. I went in and prayed with him, and saw how the little place had been stripped by want, and I know'd what a long spell he would have of it yet.

"Jem," I says, 'I'm very sorry for 'e, and I must try to help 'e a bit.'

"'Well, we musn't be sorry, Dan'el,' says he. 'It be the Lord's will, you know, and we must bear it.'

"It made me quite short-tempered to hear it. 'What!' says I, 'God's will that your landlord should let you live in a place like this, with these drains about here, poisonin' you with the stench, an' poisonin' the water you drink! It be very different from God's will, Jem. I've just a-come up over the hill side, and all the air was sweet with His own breath, furze blossoms and flowers; and then up in the clear blue sky a lark was singing lovely as ever you heard, and everything was so pretty as the Almighty Himself could make it. An' then I come in here, and I see this slimy pond, and this black drain, and I couldn't help thinkin' how different the Lord would have it. It ben't His blessed will that landlords should be misers and fools, and next door to murderers, Jem; and all the religion in the world wouldn't make me own to that.'"

Widow Pascoe actually opened her eyes, and half opened her mouth; a sufficient evidence of her amazement at such an extraordinary statement. That dirt and wretchedness were not the will of God: it smacked of heresy!

Dan'el went on again fiercely: "I can't abide to hear folks talkin' about it; puttin' down everything that is sad, and bad, and miserable, to be the Lord's will." The little eye turned its sharp glance full upon Brother Trundle. "It ben't the Lord's will, but just our own folly very often that makes the Lord deal with us a bit hardly. Fancy Eve a-comin' out of Paradise, and when the earth begins to get covered with thorns and briers, and Adam has to go earnin' his daily bread by the sweat o' his brow, she says, 'Well, you know, its the Lord's will, and we must bear it.' Not a bit of it. They knew that the Lord's will was Paradise. The Lord's will was all the fruit, and flowers, and beauty of Eden. It was right against the will of their Father that there should come these thorns and things, and weariness and sorrow; only it was just what their sins forced the Lord to do. When I was a little chap my father had to give me a thrashin' one day, and sent me up in the garret to finish the day on dry bread and water. Do you think I said, 'It's my father's will, and I must bear it.' No; I knew too much about myself to do anything like that. His will! Why I can mind now how his lip quivered, and how grieved he looked, and I knew it was all along o' my own foolin', and it just served me right.

"And if a man goes a-forgettin' his Heavenly Father and neglectin' the means in makin' money, and is comin' to love it till it be a'most chokin' the grace out of him, the Lord is forced to take some of it away, or to let him go and fling it away, which comes to just the same thing. And then the man begins to talk quite religious about *sufferin' the Lord's will!* By all means let him suffer the Lord's will, which to my thinkin' is this here,—that he shouldn't love what he has got left, and should make a better use o' what he earns another day. Why when the poor old Squire tumbled down in a fit, and the doctor bled him to bring him to his senses, he didn't talk about bearin' the doctor's will. Everybody knew that the doctor took his blood to save his life. An' seemin' to me 'twould save us a heap o' folly if we were so wise in our religion as folks be about everything else a'most.

"But this isn't the worst of it, either. I wouldn't mind so much if people put in the other side a bit; but they won't do that. No; 'tis only what's *wisht* and dismal, and ugly,—that be the Lord's will. If a man be laid 'pon his bed in a raging fever, that's the Lord's will; but if the fever don't come near to him nor to anybody else, why that's nothing at all. Poor old Uncle Jan Kevern be doubled up a'most with rheumatics; that's the Lord's will, you know. But I can stick to my last all day, and make a pair o' shoes, and nobody ever thinks that *that* is the will of our Blessed Father. I do dearly love that hundred and fourth psalm: 'My meditation of Him shall be sweet,' says David. But our meditations of Him be all that is doleful and dull. David sang about the will of the Lord when he saw the man going forth to his work, and to his labour unto the evening. *Sang* about it too. But we sigh about the Lord's will only when a man be kept home all day, or when he be a-going to die, and leave a widow and half a score o' little children. Why, bless the Lord! His will has got quite as much to do with health as with sickness, an' more too."

"Bless Him, that it have, dear leader!" responded Frankey from his corner, with much fervour.

Dan'el went on again, without fierceness now; with a gentleness and tenderness that came from his heart. "Aw, my dear friends, I often think about it when I be a-doin' up my bit o' garden down to my place. People talk as if the Blessed Master only got fruit out of us with a *prunin' knife*; always standin' over us, an' a cuttin' here, and a loppin' there. Why, bless His Name, sunshine and showers, and the gentle south winds, have a deal more to do with a bunch of grapes than prunin' knives have. We do want a bit o' prunin' now an' then, I dare say, but don't 'e go a-thinkin' about the dear Lord as only standin' over us for that. A standin' there with all his kindness and care—why He is trainin' the branches, and is watching over us, and wardin' off blights, and keepin' off enemies,—slugs, and snails, and such like, that do harbour in a man's soul; and His gentleness and loving care have a deal more to do with the fruit than the knife has.

"O, don't let us always be a-talking about bearin' His will, and sufferin' His will. Let's talk about *enjoyin'* His will. When the baby is pinin' away and sickly, an' dyin', that be His will, perhaps; but that be His will, too, when the baby be a great big thumpin' boy, and thrives uncommon. It be God's will, perhaps—if it ben't our own carelessness—when the house be burnt down, and we escape with our lives. But it be the Lord's will, too, all the days that we come and go, and find all safe and sound. The Father's will isn't that we should be out in a far country perishin' with hunger. His will is the best robe and the fatted calf; the comin' home, and the being merry. '*My meditation of Him shall be sweet.*' You may say what you like about *sufferin'* the Lord's will; I shall talk about enjoying it, and delighting in it."

"So will I, bless Him," said Frankey.

Even Widow Pascoe looked as if a little light had come across her mourning face, as that evening finished with the hymn—

> "God of my life, through all my days,
> My grateful powers shall sound Thy praise:
> My song shall wake with opening light,
> And cheer the dark and silent night.
>
> "The cheerful tribute will I give,
> Long as a deathless soul shall live:
> A work so sweet, a theme so high,
> Demands and crowns eternity."

VIII.

"Catchin' 'em with guile."

OF all the good folks in the little village of Penwinnin none was a greater favourite with Dan'el than young Cap'n Joe. His presence "at Class" had much influence on the "religious notions," and his story was one that Dan'el used to tell with unfailing pleasure.

He had begun life as a poor lad, without any advantage of education or position; rather, indeed, with all the disadvantages that could gather about him. His father was a dissolute man, whose wit had once been the life of the public-house; but that light had long since been quenched, and there was left only a bloated half-drunk idler, loafing about the public-house for any odd job that might turn up. The half-starved wife and mother lived in a wretched home, trying to bring up this only child as best she could.

But as a little lad Joe had taken a very practical view of his own case. He had nobody else to help him, and by that circumstance seemed only impelled to do so much the more to help himself. Reading and writing were soon mastered, and there early appeared the promise of what he would be.

Dan'el's quick eye had seen him in the Sunday-school; and the little cobbler's shop became in time a sort of night-school, where Joe learnt many a lesson, and picked up much good advice. He had begun as a common miner, but rose in the confidence of those about him, until now he was dignified as Cap'n Joe, an under manager of the mine, and had left his old teacher behind him in all but shrewdness and common sense.

Dan'el used to tell with much glee how young Cap'n Joe had done the Purser of the mine,—a hard, snappish, sour old screw, whose delight was in grinding everybody down.

"He came in here laughin' one evening," said Dan'el, and the little bright eye flashed with a joyous humour over the broad-rimmed spectacles.

"'Catchin' 'em with guile be scriptural, Dan'el, ben't it?' he began, and I knew there was something queer comin', but couldn't guess what it was.

"'Depends what kind o' guile it is, and what it be a-goin' to do,' I answered,—cautious, for I didn't know what was comin'.

"'Why the men up to mine have wanted a dryin'-room for ever so long, you know: comin' up hot and damp as they do; it be enough for to give 'em their death o' cold to go out ever so far in the wind and rain,' says Cap'n Joe, lookin' just as queer as he did at first.

"'That it be, Joe,' I says, ' but men be only men, you know. The Pharisees might pull out a sheep or an ox, but then they were worth something. But men are such common kind o' creatures, and so different. If they were only horses, or pigs even, folks would take some care of 'em; but they be only men, and you can't sell them, at least in this here country. Well, Joe?'

"'Well, what I do say about it be nothing at all; for the Purser will have it all his own way. He'd say "Yes," just contrairy like, if I said "No." He be like the "bob" to the engine, that do dip down just because the other end do tip up,' says the young Cap'n.

"'Well, but,' says I, 'you might speak your mind about it, Joe. It would be a comfort to give your testimony to what be right, even if nobody don't receive it. Besides, you can't shake the dust of your feet agen 'em till you have done that much.'

"'No, Dan'el, it would only harden him, and make him more determined. I've had to catch him with guile.'

"'You have?' I cried, quite curious to hear about it."

And Dan'el lifted his spectacles on to his forehead as he told of it, as if his curiosity always revived at this point by some subtle law of association.

"So then Joe told me about it," said Dan'el. "'You see,' he says, 'the men kep' on comin' to me about it: 'twas always the same thing. Till last of all, I says to 'em, "Well, look here, 'tis no good to keep tellin' me about it, men. The Purser must give the orders. But now, 'spose I say you shan't have a dryin'-room, and I won't let 'e have it, and you go up and tell the Purser what I've said." So three of 'em goes up to the office, and sees the Purser. He was oncommon cross and gruff, even for him, and so soon as they began for to speak about a dryin'-room, he gets into a rage. "Dryin'-room!" he halloos out, "I dare say you do. Umph! You'll want dinner provided next, and a champagne luncheon, I s'pose. Certainly, certainly! What next will you want, I wonder."

"'Well, Sir,' says the men, 'we spoke to young Cap'n Joe about it.'

"'O, you spoke to him did you? And what did he say?'

"'Why, he said as he wasn't a-goin' to speak to you about it at all, but would speak right off ou his own authority, and that we shouldn't have it,—*that we shouldn't.*'

"'The men say as he got into a towerin' rage. "*He* said you shouldn't!" he cries out. "Cap'n Joe, indeed! Who's *he*, I should like to know? I'll let him know who's master up here—the young upstart. Go down and tell him that I said you *should* have it,—*I said so*, and tell him to see about it at once." And they said that he went on mutterin' about it for an hour after.'

"'Well done, Joe,' says I, laughing out loud. 'Aw, 'iss, my dear, 'iss, it be quite lawful for to catch 'em with guile.'"

IX.

"Prayin' breath is never spent in vain."

"LA! what's that, my dear? 'Prayin' breath never spent in vain!'"

And there was a long pause in which the little bullet head shook itself, and the keen little eye peered over the broad-rimmed spectacles; and the honest man who had thus completed his experience looked up in some amazement that such a common phrase could be anything but Gospel.

"That ben't in the Scriptures, my dear; though I believe many folks do reckon it be. But it isn't there, and if folks would look for it they would

find something a deal truer. They would find this—
'*Ye ask, and receive not, because ye ask amiss.*'
Now I do reckon that there's a good half of the
prayin' breaths as be spent in vain. Half! why,
nearer ninety out of every hundred. What with
one thing and another that be *amiss*, it's well if one
out a hundred be worth anything at all. It be
only another o' them common sayings that be lies
that would have gone rotten and been flung away
long ago, only that there's just a grain o' the salt o'
truth in 'em to keep 'em alive.

"Why, now, *whenever we pray for what we don't
want, neither needin' it, nor desirin' to have it*, that's
a prayin' breath spent in vain. And that's more
than half our prayers. I overtook a young fellow
the other day, a good sort of a young man, too, and
I says, 'Well, John, and how's the soul prosperin'?'

"'Don't know,' says he in a melancholy kind of
a way: and the way a man talks about his soul is
more than what he says very often. Its like feelin'
the pulse and tells more than lookin' into his face.
'Don't know; reckon it be busy-all,' says he, 'to
get along.'

"'Well, now,' I said, 'just let me ask you one
question that may explain it all,—How do you pray,
John?'

"'Pray, Dan'el,' he says, wonderin', 'why the
same as other people do, to be sure—'pon my knees.'

"'Of course you do, John,' I says; 'but what do 'e say now?'" For my dear friends it be no good a-goin' hummin' and haa-in' about it. I do reckon a Class-leader be like a doctor, and he must find out what be wrong, and if he can't do it one way he must another. And he must go lookin' and listenin' and tryin' till he have found out, and then he'll have a chance o' curin'. So I says, 'Now what do 'e say?'

"'Well,' he says quite innocent, 'my mother taught me a prayer when I was a little lad, and I do say that.'

"'Why, my dear boy,' I says, 'no wonder you don't get along! Why, I expect the first thing my mother taught me to say was, "Please for a bit o' bread." Now, however should I have got along, do you think, if I'd always gone on sayin' "Please for a bit o' bread." If I wanted leather, or brad-awls, flower-seeds, or lap-stones, coats or bricks, or money, or anything else, and I'd always gone sayin' "Please for a bit o' bread."'

"'O!' says he, 'Dan'el that be very different, o' course.'

"'How different? I can't see that it's any different. I want things from folks about me, and I go and tell them what I want, and I stare if I don't get 'em. But I go to the Heavenly Father and, never mind what I want, I just go sayin' over and over the same things, and then I talk all doleful about my not gettin' on! Why whatever else can we expect?'

"John was quiet for a minute or two, and then says he, in his slow way, as if his words came out in drops because he was afraid to turn the tap, 'Well, Dan'el, I never thought o' that afore.' And he turned in over the fields.

"Now I got home, thinkin' that I had let a bit o' daylight in upon him, and then I soon found myself trippin' and came down in the dust. I was kneelin' down at prayer, and my thoughts began to go away to John again, my lips goin' on all the time. And when my thoughts came back again there was I going over an old sentence about forgivin' the sins o' the day. I stopped. 'O, Dan'el,' I says out loud, 'you be a pretty kind of a teacher to talk to other people about prayin' for what they want! Physician, heal thyself! What sins do you want forgiven? and if you want 'em forgiven, do you believe you are goin' to get it by saying a phrase like that, as smooth and pat as anything.' 'Lord forgive me,' I says with all my heart. And I began to look about through the day to find what I did want. And I soon found it, my friends, a deal sooner than I thought I should. About eleven o'clock in the mornin' it was; I mind it quite well, —there was a pair o' shoes to be done for a man that was goin' away to California, and things had been goin' wrong all day, and I had to send down to Redburn for something, and the boy kept me waitin' and then brought back all wrong, and I got in a temper with him and spoke out sharp, and said a deal more than I ought to have said, and felt a good deal more than come out. 'There, Dan'el,' I says, 'you need forgiveness for *that*. Repent and pray about *that*.' Why it was like another thing then. It began to hurt me, and the tears began to flow, and I meant it then when I got down before the Lord and prayed that I might be forgiven. And I got forgiven, too; and the next day when I came down I called the boy over to me and I told him that I was ashamed of myself for the way I had gone on the day before, an' I hoped he'd forgive me for I was very sorry. As to the boy, why I never knew a boy change so in my life as that changed him: seemin' to me as if he can't ever be thoughtful and steady enough now. Ah, my friends, that be the kind of breath that ben't spent in vain! When a man feels it, and can put his hand right upon the spot and say, 'Lord, *'tis amiss just there*, and 'tis hurting me and plaguin' more than I can bear,—Lord, do it good.' Then that goes right up to heaven."

"We can manage that when we feel anything deeply, my dear leader," said young Cap'n Joe, from his place. "Jacob prayed like that when he was a-goin' to meet Esau. But I've wondered how he prayed next day when it was all quiet again and there was nothing particular hangin' over him!"

"Yes, yes, Cap'n Joe," said Dan'el thoughtfully, "there be a deal in that. Well, Frankey, my dear, tell us how you do manage," and Dan'el turned with a loving reverence to the old man.

"Me, my dear leader, why I ha'an't got much to tell. Seemin' to me 'tis like this here. When I do kneel down, I do think, and feel it too,—Well, here be another day, an' I don't know what'll happen, but right over it all there be the wings o' my Father in Heaven, and all day long I shall be in under them there wings, and no harm can't come to me in there—bless His holy Name. And my heart do begin to sing again and goes on singin' all day long. An' then when the night be come again I do think, and feel too, like as if the wings was foldin' in round me, and I put myself in under them, and I do feel such a blessed rest in under there—like as if it were so safe and so warm and so comfortable,— nothing couldn' hurt me, in there, ne'er man nor devil. Bless His holy Name!"

"Well, Frankey, I do think you've got hold o' the right thing after all. *Thinkin'* about it beforehand, fixin' your thoughts 'pon it. Why, we pray like we don't do anything else in the world. There be plenty o' fools that go a-shootin'—poppin' at the larks, an' blackbirds, and thrushes, like as if they didn't sing for their supper an' more than pay for all the harm they do. But I never heard tell of a fool who fired his gun without any aim; fired it off anyhow and anywhere, and then expected to see the bird fall. But that be just like we pray. We don't *take aim*. We don't think beforehand. Frankey here, have explained it, 'xactly, seemin' to me. Now, suppose to-morrow mornin' we kneel down, and begin to think: To-day where am I goin' to? what shall I be a-doin' of? What grace shall I need? Where'll the devil be lying-wait for me? Thoughts 'll come—they 'll come, and we shall begin to find out needs enough to pray about. Why, I could a'most pray now as I come to think about it. Why there be that Particular Baptist who comes droppin' in 'pon a Wednesday, and we begin a argufyin' 'pon Calvinism, and Wesley and Fletcher, and I do a'most always get hot and angry and vexed with myself—I'll aim straight at him to-morrow, that I will! That is it, my friends. Think what you do want beforehand, and then you won't go a-wasting your breath in prayin' for what you don't want.

"Then there be another prayin' breath that be spent in vain. When we *go a-prayin' for what we don't expect*. That be in vain—and that'll cover a'most the other half of our prayers. '*Believin'* ye *receive,'*—that be the pith and marrow o' prayer, in my thinkin'. But we pray, and don't ever look for it to come down; like a man takin' aim and shooting, but never goin' in to pick up what he's shot. '*I will direct my prayer unto Thee, and will look up.*' That be the way David prayed. He took aim and expected to see the blessings come down. We don't expect to get our prayers answered."

"Like as if He didn't mean what He said in all the precious promises: bless Him!" came fervently from dear old Frankey in the corner.

"I've often thought how folks would stare, sometimes, if their prayers were answered," said young Cap'n Joe.

Dan'el smiled, as if some slumbering memory woke up suddenly within him. He nodded the little head, and the merry wrinkles gathered round the corner of the bright eye, and the pursed-up mouth.

"They would, sure 'nough, Cap'n Joe. I happened once to be stayin' with a gentleman,—a long way from here,—a very religious kind of a man he was; and in the mornin' he began the day with a long family prayer that we might be kep' from sin, and might have a Christ-like spirit, and the mind that was also in Christ Jesus; and that we might have the love of God shed abroad in our hearts by the Holy Ghost given unto us. A beautiful prayer it was, and thinks I, what a good kind of a man you must be. But about an hour after I happened to be comin' along the farm, and I heard him hollerin' and scoldin' and goin' on findin' fault with everybody and everything. And when I came into the house with 'en he began again. Nothing was right, and he was so impatient and so quick-tempered. '"Tis very provokin' to be annoyed in this way, Dan'el. I don't know what servants in these times be good for but to worry and vex one, with their idle, slovenly ways.'

"I didn't say nothing for a minute or two. And then I says, 'You must be very much disappointed, Sir.'

"'How so, Dan'el? Disappointed?

"'I thought you were expecting to receive a very valuable present this morning, Sir, and I see it hasn't come.'

"'Present, Dan'el,'—and he scratched his head, as much as to say, 'whatever can the man be talkin' about.'

"'I certainly heard you speakin' of it, Sir,' I says, quite coolly.

"'Heard me speak of a valuable present. Why, Dan'el you must be dreamin.' I've never thought of such a thing.'

"'Perhaps not, Sir, but you've talked about it; and I hoped it would come whilst I was here, for I should dearly like to see it.'

"He was gettin' angry with me now, so I thought I would explain.

"'You know, Sir, this mornin' you prayed for a Christ-like spirit, and the mind that was in Jesus, and the love of God shed abroad in your heart.?

"'O, that's what you mean is it!' and he spoke as if that weren't anything at all.

"'Now, Sir, wouldn't you be rather surprised if your prayer was to be answered? If you were to feel a nice, gentle, lovin' kind of a spirit comin' down upon you, all patient, and forgivin' and kind? Why, Sir, wouldn't you come to be quite frightened like; and you'd come in and sit down all in a faint, and reckon as you must be a-goin' to die, because you felt so heavenly-minded?'

"He didn't like it very much," said Dan'el, "but I delivered my testimony, and learnt a lesson for myself too. You're right, Cap'n Joe; you're right. We should stare very often if the Lord was to answer our prayer. That sayin' won't hold water no more than any o' the rest,—a prayin breath be very often spent in vain."

X.

"A talk to the Lambs."

T must not be thought that my dear old friend was always on the lookout for these religious proverbs, having no eyes or ears for anything else—like a cat watching for the unsuspecting mouse, and then springing upon it to tear it to pieces. True he treated these phrases in this style, and with a manifest relish; but many an evening passed without any such destruction of the prey, when there was just as much homely common-sense and helpful advice.

To the young and to the old there was a peculiar tenderness, perhaps especially to the old folks. "Seemin' to me that the two dearest things in all the world to our Heavenly Father be a little child and an old saint," was a favourite saying with Dan'el; a saying to which dear old Frankey Vivian usually responded in a look beaming with joy, and a fervent "Bless His dear Name for that!"

The previous winter had brought many additions to Dan'el's Classes, mostly of young folks, whom he welcomed very heartily, and made them feel as much at home as anybody else. Dear old Granny Toms herself was sometimes pulled up when she was running on too long, with a hint that she must leave time for "a word to the young uns." Widow Pascoe was sometimes startled by the question if she had something bright to give them to encourage the lambs,—a question which seemed to give her "quite a turn;" but the folded hands and the tucked-down mouth regained their propriety, and in a moment she recovered her self-possession. The word exactly hits it,—*self-possession* was Widow Pascoe's ruin, as it is the ruin of thousands of us. "Possessed of the devil was a misfortune and to be pitied," said Dan'el one day as we talked of it, "but *possessed of ourselves* is a curse and a misery that ben't much above it. There is only one possession that God's people should know anything about, and that is *Christ in us*, the hope of glory."

He very seldom asked these younger members to speak. "God lets the children learn to live a bit and to walk a bit by theirselves before He lets 'em talk," was his explanation. Hurrying through the rest of the Class, or contenting himself with speaking to three or four of the members, he would reserve a quarter of an hour for "a word to the lambs."

It was an evening in May when the setting sun flung in its ruddy light upon the happy company at Thomas Toms'. Stretching the neck you could look over the muslin blind that cut the window in two, and catch sight of Farmer Gribble's fields beyond, with the sheep and lambs luxuriating in the rich green grass and golden buttercups. The scene may have suggested the talk of that evening.

"Ah! young folks, you've got a blessed Saviour, you have. When I begin to think about it I a'most wish that I could go back and be a little child again. Why you know *He carries the lambs in His bosom.* Wonderful, but true. *Carries* them! It doesn't matter much what the road is when we are carried,—highway or by-way, field-path or muddy lane, it be all as one to them that are being carried, and it don't matter how weak you are, or how foolish; you can't get tired, and you can't miss the way when you're being carried. He—that's *your* Saviour—carries the lambs—that's *you*, your very self—in His bosom.

"Now think about yourselves as lambs—young uns—who don't know the way, an' don't know the dangers, an' go a-friskin' out o' the way a'most before you know you're in it; lambs that can't keep up with the old ones, and it ben't natural as you should; lambs so easily frightened that you're scared when the shepherd comes to count you and see that you are all right, and yet so ignorant that you'll go rubbin' your noses against the butcher's greasy knee when he comes to buy you. And so the devil comes a-whisperin', an' says he, 'Pooh, you're a-settin' out for the kingdom, and hopin' to get to heaven. You can't do it, a little silly lamb like you. Wait; there's no need to hurry. Wait till you are grown up a steady-going old sheep. Why there's the rest o' the lambs a-friskin' about among the buttercups and daisies, as happy as the day is long, and here you'll be goin' to Class-meetin', a-mopin' about among the nettles, and trying to look solemn and to cry like an old ewe that has lost her little one, and to be so proper as if you're much too good to jump about and enjoy yourself. You wait till you be grown up.' That's how he talks, the old liar.

"'Then,' says he, 'there's the wolf that's about, and he may have you; and how the folks 'll talk about it,—you settin' yourself up for a member, like as if you'd be so much better than everybody else, and the wolf gettin' you after all, just the same as if you'd been a wild wanderin' lamb all the time.'

"'That's how he talks. I do hate 'en, for comin' so to you young ones. If he'd come and have a bout with an old soldier like me it wouldn't be so bad, but to come a-bullyin' and a-frightenin' you—it is such a bit o' ghastly old cowardice as anybody else would be ashamed of. But theare, it be like 'en all over. And he comes round pratin' again: 'It be a hard road to go up, and choke-full o' troubles and trials. And the devil will set snares an' traps and pitfalls for 'e; an' there be gloomy woods, an' desert places, and swellin's o' Jordan, and great cities wall'd up to heaven, and ugly great sons of Anak.' Poor little lamb, I don't wonder that thee'rt most afeared to set out. But don't listen to him. Don't take one bit o' notice o' what he says. See, here is thy tender Shepherd standin' over thee, and lookin' down upon thee with all His pitiful love. 'Poor little lamb,' He saith, 'fear not, I will carry thee in My bosom.' And he puts His hand in under thee, and He lifts thee up into His arms, and *He carries the lamb in His bosom.*

There's pretty ridin' for thee now, little one. Bless His dear Name! What now of mopin' among the nettles? What now of the wolf? I see him go sneakin' off with his tail between his legs, and his eyes glistenin' green with sick envy. He can't touch thee there, in thy Saviour's bosom. What now o' desert places, and gloomy woods, and mountains o' difficulty. He *carries* the lambs. 'Wait till thou art grown up!' Why that would be to lose it all. Thou art so blest because thou art so little; thou art so safe because thou art so weak. He carries the lambs."

"Bless Thy dear Name," came from Frankey's corner, where the shadows of evening now began to gather thickly.

"But that be not all, though it be a good deal," Dan'el went on again. "He carries them in *His bosom—in His bosom.* You know the man who had a hundred sheep and lost one of them, went after it,—I dare say with his dog that scented it out and found it in the ditch, bramble-torn and wasted, and that barked at it, and grabbed at its wool, and drove it roughly to the shepherd. And the shepherd laid it on *His shoulders—on His shoulders.* When an old sheep goes astray—one of us old uns, the Good Shepherd has His watch dog to fetch us back again. He sends a snappish sorrow to bite us, or a sharp-toothed loss to shake us up a bit and to drive us out of the ditch into which we had wandered."

Dan'el's little eye shot its glance across to John Trundle, who shook his head as much as to say—"That's true." Widow Pascoe sighed deeply.

"And serve us right too," Dan'el went on, "serve us right. Old sheep like we are—what do we want, goin' astray and tumblin' into ditches. Serve us right. We ought to know better, and deserve that the watch-dog should give us a bite that'll be a warnin' to us for all the rest of our days. And the shepherd lays the runaway on his shoulder. It wasn't a very comfortable position, held on by the legs, with his head danglin' down, and all the rest of the sheep comin' round him, thinkin' what a figure he looked. That be the way the Lord carries us old sheep when we go astray. He brings us back makin' us feel uncomfortable, and very much ashamed of ourselves. But the lambs He carries *in His bosom—in His bosom*. The shoulder is not for them but the bosom. There they lie, with His arms folded about them—there, where His kind eye can keep its glance upon them. In His bosom—where they can feel the great full heart beatin' in its love, where He can hear the first mutter o' their fear, and they can catch the gentlest whisper of His lovin' care. He carries the lambs in His bosom. Keep close to Him—lie down in His arms, an' you're safe enough.

"Don't go thinkin' about yourself—you're weak, of course you are—you're ignorant, of course you are. And so the Shepherd will take all the more care of you for that. Don't let that scare us, or let it scare us only into our Saviour's arms. I was down under the cliffs the other day, and there was a man there with his two boys and a little girl. The boys were strong lusty fellows, who could run down the steep path and leap over the rocks like young goats. But the little maid was lame. And you should have seen that father helpin' her because she was lame. How carefully he led her along, an' how he lifted her over the stones, and how gently he brought her on step by step till at last he set her to sit upon a rock, and she leaned against him. Then as she looked out upon the blue ocean, and on the cliffs, an' the white gulls wheelin' up above her, an' the ships far out at sea—she enjoyed it all so much that tears o' very joy came into the father's eyes. Ah, bless the Lord, that be just like Him! The strong lusty ones can get on perhaps—though He won't let *them* out of His sight. But the lame and the weak, and the little ones, how gently He leads them, how He takes them on a step at a time —how tenderly He lifts them over the rough places, and then how He delights to lead us to some cleft in the rock and there to make all His goodness to pass before us!"

Dan'el paused. The tenderness and touching way in which he had spoken had more to do with it perhaps than the words themselves, but there was not a heart there that had not been moved to tears. And the general feeling found a relief in dear old Frankey's fervent words: "Bless His dear Name! It be true, my dear leader, every word of it. Bless Him! And not only for the lambs of the flock. I've been a-thinkin' o' them words: '*Even to your old age I am He; and even to hoar hairs will I carry you.*'"

But Dan'el had not finished his talk, and quietly went on again.

"And yet mind you're *lambs*. Though you be in the dear Lord's bosom you're lambs—not old sober-sided sheep that have got no friskin' in them. God made the lambs to leap about, you know. And you are His lambs. Don't think that it is a sin to laugh or to play or to be as happy and as merry as lambs in the fields. I am quite sure that God's people are very often the devil's shepherds, —without knowin' it of course,—and do a deal o' harm to the lambs o' the fold. I know that about a fortnight after I had found the love of God to me in Christ Jesus, one day my soul was full o' love an' joy an' gratitude, and I was workin' away as happy as could be, when the devil came to me and whispers,—'Dan'el, if you go on like this, you'll die and go to heaven like such good people always do, and then what'll come to your mother and who'll keep the place over her head?'

"I was foolish enough to listen to him for a minute or two, but that was enough. I jumped up from my work and rolled my apron around my waist, and I ran across the road. There before me was old Farmer Gribble's gate—a five-barred gate. So I took a run and leaped over that half-a-dozen times, and the last time I tumbled over it and bruised my shin. So I came back limpin' to my work and sat down again. 'Theare,' I said, 'that'll settle that anyhow: who ever heard of anybody dyin' while they could jump over a five-barred gate like that, or who ever went to heaven while he could bruise his shin in that style?'

"Well, I thought that was a pretty way o' jumpin' out o' the snare. But I found that I'd only jumped out o' the fryin'-pan into the fire. For the next day I went to Class, and an old man—he's in heaven now—began quite solemn, and turnin' a look upon me that made me feel dreadfully guilty,—'How some folks can make a profession o' religion, an' do as they do, be more 'an I can understand, goin' and jumpin' over a five-barred gate like as if 'twas the whole ten comman'ments at a stride. An' not once, nor yet twice, but agen an' agen, till last of all the judgments o' heaven come down an' a'most broke his leg!'

"I went home thinkin' myself a dreadful sinner, and if my dear mother hadn't had so much sense I should have given up in despair, and have thought that there was no chance for anybody so wicked as I was. When I told her about it she smiled,— ah! I think I can hear her still in her gentle, quiet way,—'I am glad thee can jump so well, Dan'el,' she says; 'but to-morrow go and jump a gate where the old man can't see thee, for we must not offend the conscience of a weak brother you know, —and see that thou does n' bruise thy shin so badly next time.'

"You're lambs, you young folks, you're lambs, and don't go tryin' to be old sheep. You're lambs —only lambs—though He does carry you in His bosom."

XL.

"Trustin' Him where we cannot trace Him."

THUS Widow Pascoe had finished her doleful statement.

She had picked out all the mysteries and perplexities of her lot. She had sighed, with a sigh that spoke volumes, over a list of her troubles and trials. She had gone through a very dismal catalogue of the ills of the past. She had languidly shut her eyes, as if by way of adding to that darkness which was to her the emblem of true religion, and had shaken her head very solemnly over the fears of the future. As to love and joy and deliverance, she had not a word from beginning to end. Of Him Who always *"causeth us to triumph;"* through Whom we are *"more than conquerors,"* there was just one word at the last: in a tone of despair she wound up by saying, *she hoped she should trust Him where she could not trace Him.* Then her mouth returned to its sour propriety, drawn down at the corners and tucked in under the folds that kept it in its place.

Poor Dan'el! More than once he had rushed at this sentence, and hacked and hewed it till he hoped it was past recovery; but here it was, growing luxuriant as ever in the garden, or rather in the graveyard of Widow Pascoe's soul. Again Dan'el gathered his strength to demolish it. Yet it was with much tenderness, and almost sadness, that he began,—

"Trust Him where? Trust Him *where you cannot trace Him!* Why, of course, of course: you know you can't trust Him anywhere else. You didn't mean any harm, I know. Folks mostly never do mean any harm; but they do it for all that. One way not to do any harm, is not to say any harm. If we thought more about what we *said*, we shouldn't do so much harm by a good deal.

"Trust Him where you cannot trace Him! Why he's a very poor creature amongst us that you can't say that much of. If you haven't got any confidence in a man, you can't say much worse of him than this—'I'll trust him as far as I can see.' The other day a neighbour of mine was a bit hard up, and he came in to my place, and told me of it. Well, I knew that he was a good kind of a man, so I let him have a sovereign. I gave him the money and away he went. Now suppose that as soon as he had turned his back I began to think about my money. Come, I say to myself, I'll trust him where I cannot trace him: but where I can trace him, what should I trust him for? So I slip out after him. He goes down the road, and I am at his heels: he turns in over the fields, and I am after him: he goes up the lane, and I keep my eye upon him; and then he turns into his house, and shuts the door. So I sit down on the doorstep, and console myself with the saying, 'Well, I can't trace him any further, so now I must trust him.' There I sit hour after hour *trustin'* him. By-and-by he comes out and finds me there.

"'Why, Dan'el, what are you a-doin' of here?' says he.

"'O,' says I, quite coolly, 'trustin' thee, neighbour, trustin' thee where I cannot trace thee.'

"Now wouldn't he get very angry, and cry out, 'Is that what you call trustin' me! a-followin' me about in that fashion? Here, take the sovereign back again. I can starve, but I can't be doubted and suspected.'

"Why, it's about as bad as you can serve anybody, only to trust 'em because you cannot trace them. And to hope for grace to treat our lovin' Father like that! You didn't mean it, I'm sure. Bless His holy Name; it hurts me somehow to think anything like that about my blessed Father, and much more to hear people keep sayin' it.

"*Trustin' Him where we cannot trace Him!* Why, it be a poor kind o' trust that only trusts because it is blind, and not because it has got any faith in them that lead it; to go on wonderin' and doubtin' and fearin', a-reaching out the hand, and a-feelin' with the foot, as if them that lead haven't a bit more eyesight than the blind man himself. When I was a little lad I remember once I'd gone up to spend the day with my grandmother. About sunset, when I ought to be goin' home, there came a tremendous thunderstorm, and the rain came down in torrents. Of course I couldn't start when it was like that, so my old grandmother said: 'Dan'el, my lad, however wilt thee get home?' And just as she was talkin', in came my father, drippin' wet. He had on a great long blue cloak, like they used to wear in those times. So when we started to come away, he said, 'Now, Dan'el, come in under here;' and he put me inside the long cloak. I got in under there, and took hold of his hand, and away we went. It was pitch dark in there, o' course, and outside I could hear the thunder crashin' about among the hills, and every now and then I took hold of his hand tighter, for somehow I could see the blaze o' the lightnin' right in under the cloak. I went splashin' on through the puddles and the mud, all right because I'd got hold of his hand. Now shouldn't I have been a little stupid if I'd kept a-sayin', 'I don't know where I'm goin' to, and I can't tell where I am, and I can't see the way, and it's very dark, and I must trust my father where I cannot trace him.'

"Why I didn't grumble at the darkness; it would be like grumblin' at my father's cloak that wrapped me from the storm. I knew that he knew the way right enough. He looked out, and managed to see the road somehow. And at last we stopped at our door; and they flung back the cloak, and there I was in front o' the blazin' fire, with mother gettin' us all sorts o' dry things, and the supper waitin', and all lookin such a welcome,—like only a lad's mother can give him. Of course he led me home: where else should he lead me too? An' seemin' to me that be just the way it ought to be with our Heavenly Father."

"Under the very shadow o' His wing, dear leader. He do love to cover us with His feathers, bless Him," said old Frankey fervently.

"Under His wing, my dear Frankey. And in

there we don't mind the dark a bit. It's so safe, an' so warm; so snug. We can take His hand, and then go 'long our way rejoicin'. What of a few splashy puddles under-foot; and a bit of a storm now and then! Why we'll only take hold of His hand all the tighter. Of course we don't know the way, and don't want to either. Our Father looks out all along the way; and He leads us right. Aye, and by-and-by we'll get to the door; an' then we'll step out into the light, and be safe home, leavin' all the wild storms and darkness outside for ever and ever: and what more can anybody want than that? Goin' a-tracin' Him, like as if He didn't know; or like as if we weren't quite sure that He was takin' us right. Where else will the Father lead us but to the Father's house, I should like to know?"

"Bless His dear Name," cried Frankey; "straight home, o' course, straight home;" and the fire-light glistened in the tears of joy, and made his face yet more radiant.

"Seemin' to me that trust,—that be worth the name of trust,—don't think about itself one bit: it just *feels* so safe that it don't think of askin' any questions about it. When my neighbour had my sovereign, if I hadn't trusted him I should have gone thinkin' about it, and hopin' it was all right; but because I did trust him, I sat down and went on hammerin' and stitchin' as if he had never come. O, dear folks, let us give ourselves right up to the good Lord, once for all; and then be so sure of His love an' care that we go singin' on all day long, doin' nothing else but lovin' and servin' Him with all our hearts! If we trust Him at all we shall trust Him so much that we shan't think about it enough to try and trace Him."

So Dan'el had finished. But the topic was a favourite one, and was taken up again and again. Scarcely a member but had some incident to tell; some deliverance wrought; some joy brightened by trust in the Lord. And when it came to dear old Frankey's turn, his pale worn face was lit up with holy joy and rapture.

"You've been talkin' about trustin' in the Lord where we cannot trace Him. Well, bless His dear Name, I don't know anything about tracin' Him, and I never thought anything about that. But I do love to think about *trustin'* Him, and I do know something about that, bless Him. I be a poor ignorant scholar, and always seem to be down to the bottom of the class in a good many things. But, bless Him, I've had enough, I reckon, to make me a'most the top o' the class in trustin' Him. Ah, dear leader, it be 'zackly as you been a-sayin',—so safe that you don't think 'pon it: just lyin' down in His arms, without a morsel o' care or frettin', but feeling so sure that everything be as right as it can be, an' never a shadow o' fear come creepin' up between His sunshine and me. Why if heaven be any better than that, then heaven must be a wonderful place sure 'nough. It come to my mind a week or two ago, so full an' sweet an' precious, that I can hardly think o' anything else. It was during them cold North-east winds; they had made my cough very bad, and I was shook all to bits, and felt very ill. My wife was sittin' by my side; and once when I'd had a sharp fit of it, she put down her work and looked at me till her eyes filled with tears, and says she, 'Frankey, Frankey, whatever will become of us when you be gone!'

"She was makin' a warm petticoat for the little maid; so after a minute or two I took hold of it, and I says—'What are 'e makin' my dear?'

"She held it up without a word; her heart was too full to speak.

"'For the little maid?' I says—'and a nice warm thing too. How comfortable it will keep her. Does she know about it?'

"'Know about it! why o' course not,' said the wife wondering. 'What should she know about it for?'

"I waited another minute, and then I said, 'What a wonderful mother you must be, wifie, to think about the little maid like that.'

"'Wonderful, Frankey? Why it would be

more like wonderful if I forgot that the cold weather was a-comin', and that the little maid would be a-wantin' something warm.'

"So then, you see, I had got her, my friends," and Frankey smiled.

"'O, wifie,' says I, 'do you think you be goin' to care for the little maid like that, and your Father in Heaven be a-goin' to forget you altogether! Come now, bless Him, isn't He as much to be trusted as you are? And do you think He'd see the winter comin' up sharp and cold, and not have something waitin' for you, and just what you want too? And I know, dear wife, that you wouldn't like to hear the little maid go a-frettin' and sayin' 'There, the cold winter be a-comin', and whatever shall I do if my mother should forget me.' Why you'd be hurt and grieved that she should doubt you like that. She knows that you care for her, and what more does she need to know—that's enough to keep her from frettin' about anything. *Your Heavenly Father knoweth that ye have need of all these things.* That be put down in His book for *you*, wifie, and a-purpose for *you*, and you grieve and hurt Him when you go a-frettin' about the future and doubtin' His love.'

"'Ah, Frankey, I wish I had your faith,' says she. And I let her go on with her work, hopin' she would think it over.

"When the little maid came home from school that afternoon, she had a bit of a sick headache. She went frettin' about the kitchen whilst her mother was gettin' the tea, and couldn' rest quiet for a minute together. But when the wife sat down, the little maid came and laid herself in her mother's arms, and put her head on her bosom; and her mother began to sing a quiet kind o' hymn to her. Then the little maid forgot her frettin', and sank down all snug and comfortable, and in a few minutes she was gone off to sleep. 'Frankey,' I says to myself as I looked at it, 'there's a lesson for thee. Sometimes the children o' the Heavenly Father get all fretful and sickly, and they go here and there and can't find a comfortable place anywhere, but are all nervous and fidgety. Here's what thou must do, Frankey. Thou must come and lay thyself down in the everlastin' Arms, and lean thy tired head upon the bosom of thy dear Lord, and draw His love in all round thee; and a'most before thou know it, all thy fears and troubles shall be hushed off to sleep, and thou'lt hear nothing but a quiet kind o' singin' in thy soul tellin' of His love.' Ah, it be more than true, truer than any words can tell or anybody can think for—*like as a father* (or a *mother* either) *pitieth his children, so the Lord pitieth them that fear Him.*

"It be a poor thing to go a tracin' Him. But

it be a blessed thing, sure 'nough, to put your trust in Him. And I can't understand how anybody can help a-doin' of it. Why, when things have come to the worst, and I do know what that be—when the money been done, and the cupboard been empty, and I have'nt seen a way out of my trouble, and the devil has come a temptin'—for he do love to hit a man when he's down—I've gone 'pon my knees, just like as if I got down under the Cross for a bit o' shelter from the storm. An' whichever way the wind blow, a man can get shelter there. Well, let me lift my eyes to Jesus, and see Him there for me, with the crown of thorns, an' the nails in His blessed hands and feet, and very soon my heart be so full as ever it can hold. 'Eh, Frankey,' I cry out, 'the King o' glory died for thee—died like that. One drop of His precious blood is more than all worlds, but for thee His heart emptied itself. *He gave Himself for me.*'" The old man's voice grew hoarse with deep emotion as he went on: "Why I kiss those bleeding feet, and every bit o' life and strength in me cries out 'My dear Lord, I can starve, I can suffer, I can die. But there be one thing I can never do; never —never—never. My Lord, *I can never doubt Thy love!*'"

Frankey's deep feeling filled every heart—as if indeed it were more than full, the feeling of the little company seemed almost naturally to overflow in the words which Dan'el gave out. "Let us sing a verse or two, and we will go on again.

> 'I rest beneath the' Almighty's shade :
> My griefs expire, my troubles cease :
> Thou, Lord, on Whom my soul is stay'd,
> Wilt keep me still in perfect peace.
>
> 'Me for Thine own Thou lov'st to take,
> In time and in eternity :
> Thou never, never wilt forsake
> A helpless worm that trusts in Thee.'

"The Lord bless thee, Frankey," cried Dan'el. "I'm a'most glad that you're shut up as you are with nothing to do but to think over His love, and to come and tell us about it. You've done my heart good, anyhow. But I've had my say. Come, Cap'n Joe, thou hast been thinkin' over it a bit, an' we must have a word from thee."

"Well, friends," said young Cap'n Joe in his brave, outspoken manner and with his ringing bass voice, like some sturdy David giving testimony after an old silver-haired Samuel, "I've been reminded of two or three things while I've been listenin' to-night. I've been thinkin' how much people lose by trying to trace the Lord instead of trusting Him. The other day I was on the other side of Redburn and I overtook a man who wanted to know the way. I told him I was going in sight of the place, and would show him the nearest path to it. We turned off the high-road through the wood and over the downs. The day was beautiful, and as we came along under the trees I thought I had never seen anything more lovely—the sun coming in through the leaves here and there on the branches and trunks of the trees, and lighting up the flowers, and the birds singing all about us, and the rabbits kept running across the mossy path. But that man didn't see a bit of it; not a bit. The path went winding along, and he kept putting his head first on this side and then on that to see it, and when the trees seemed to block it in, he stopped and said quite timidly: 'I'm afraid we're wrong; the pathway ends here.' I laughed at his foolishness. 'Why, I've been along here many times,' I said. 'You needn't be distressed.' But he was as nervous as ever. Then we left the wood and came out on the downs. And when we came to the top I stayed to look away over the furze and the old granite rocks to the sea. 'There's Saint Michael's Mount,' I said, pointing away in the distance. 'Isn't this a fine view?' But he looked about quite timidly and said, 'I hope we are right.'

"So I thought it was no good trying to interest him in the scenery, and I showed him the smoke of Redburn just down under us, and he thanked me and went away down the valley. I came along thinking how much these poor timid souls do lose, and how foolish it was for him to be so afraid when I'd been over the path scores of times. And I said to myself, 'That's the way with hundreds of folks going heavenwards. They forget that their Lord has led thousands of pilgrims to the Celestial City, and they come all along the way wondering if they're right, and when they stand upon the Delectable Mountains and have the stretch of beautiful scenery about them, they are timidly fearing lest they should have lost the way. I'm sure that it is a poor unhappy kind of religion—this tracing kind. Frankey's is the right sort—trust, simple trust, that feels so safe that it never thinks about it.'

"It might cure us to think what a set of ignorant creatures we are, and what mistakes we keep making when we think we can trace Him—mistakes that I reckon will be almost enough to spoil heaven itself when we wake up and find out how we've wronged our Blessed Father. There was Jacob, he tried his hand at tracing the Lord, and a mess he made of it, making himself and everybody else miserable for half a life time: going away now and then to the secret place where he kept the coat of many colours: taking it out all stained with faded marks of blood; going over the story again, shaking his head and saying bitterly, 'Doubtless some evil beast hath devoured him. I'll go sorrowing down to my grave.' And the old man goes in and out, refusing to be comforted, tearing the wound open again when it did begin to heal, and loving to have it festering. And there all the time his Father in heaven was preparing to feed them all and keep them alive in time of famine. If Jacob was like me, I know he'd feel dreadfully ashamed of himself when he got down to the land of Goshen and found his son there, the great man of the land, and he would go grieving then that he had gone grumbling before.

"That is what comes of tracing the Lord, and it must always be so, I think, for we see only one side of it—we can't see the Lord's side. Here's the coat we wanted to wrap Joseph in—right before our eyes; but we don't see the fine linen and the royal robes that are being woven down yonder in Egypt. Here's the empty chair"—for a moment Capt'n Joe's voice faltered; the grave was not yet green in which he had laid his bright-eyed eldest boy—"Here's the empty chair," he went on, "and the place where he used to sit, but we can't see the throne that God is leading him up to. It is so with all that God takes away. Our eyes are upon our lost, and we think of what is gone, but we don't see that God has taken them away only to enrich them and enrobe them with majesty and splendour, and one day to give them back to us exalted and enriched as kings and priests. We can't afford to go tracing the Lord: we make such bungling work of it.

"And talking about Jacob brings to my mind the way people go wondering what they'll do if all kinds of troubles come upon them—losses and sorrows and death. Jacob had lessons enough, as Frankey says, to teach him the blessedness of trusting the Lord. There was Esau coming up to him with a great company of armed men. He was dreadfully frightened, for the fierce hunter had been cruelly and foully wronged, and now he would surely avenge himself. And Jacob began to trace things. He couldn't have seen anything else than this, look as long as he would: his flocks and herds seized, his sons carried into slavery, and himself slain. And at last here they were right before him, the hundreds of spearmen, fierce fellows whose eyes shone at the sight of so much plunder. And Jacob came up bowing and trembling and saying, '*My lord*' and '*my lord*.' But Esau ran, generous man that he was, and fell on his brother's neck and kissed him, and wept with very joy and pressed him to come and dwell with him in his own country. Where Jacob traced destruction he found loving welcome and blessing; where he traced loss and death, he found a brother's love and a wonderful deliverance. That's the way with us. We can only see the fierce Esaus, armed and angry that are coming to slay us. But the Lord can touch the heart with his finger; and turned in a moment, it is all love and peace and blessing. We can't afford to go tracing Him; we can't afford to do anything else but trust in Him.

"Besides, when we go tracing Him, there's one thing we never see, and that makes all the difference in the world: *we never see the special grace that our good Lord will give for special seasons.* Seeming to me that these people that are always wondering what they'll do if such and such things happen, want to have the grace *now* for all their lifetime. The children of this world are wiser than the children of light, in this too, as in a good many other things."

"Aye: that be true," interrupted Dan'el somewhat fiercely, with a look as if the little eye had shot out a lightning flash, and this was the attendant thunder. "Men never are such fools anywhere as they be in religion."

Cap'n Joe continued, "For folks to keep on wondering what they'll do in the future is just as if you were to meet a man going to work with a sack of flour on his back, and a stone of meat, and a bundle of clothes. 'You know,' he says, 'I shall be hungry in three months' time, and I shall want food and clothes then, so I carry it all with me.' Now nobody was ever mazed enough to do that. The man just takes his day's dinner with him and goes to his day's work; and he believes that where to-day's meal came from, to-morrow's will too. And that is what we want. The Lord gives us one day's grace for one day's need; and to-morrow's supply will come out of the same fulness, and what more can anybody want!"

Dan'el finished the talk of the evening.

"Well, friends, 'tis a pity that the time be gone; but I must tell 'e a little story I heard the other day. Cap'n Joe been talkin' about temptations. Why, however we can listen to the devil when he do come round temptin' of us to doubt our Father's love and care, is wonderful. It be such impudence,—such down-right, brazen-faced impudence."

"Just like 'en though, my dear leader," put in Frankey.

"But I was goin' to tell the story that I heard from dear old Billy Bray. He was preachin' about temptations, and this is what he said :—

"Friends, last week I was a-diggin' up my 'taturs. It was a wisht poor yield, sure 'nough : there was hardly a sound one in the whole lot. An' while I was a-diggin' the devil come to me, and he says, 'Billy, do you think your Father do love you?'

"I should reckon He do," I says.

"'Well, I don't,' says the ould tempter in a minute. If I'd thought about it I shouldn't ha' listened to 'en, for his 'pinions ben't worth the leastest bit o' notice. 'I don't,' says he, 'and I tell 'ee what for: if your Father loved you, Billy Bray, He'd give you a pretty yield o' 'taturs; so much as ever you do want, and ever so many of 'em, and every one of 'em as big as your fist. For it ben't no trouble for your Father to do anything; and He could just as easy give you plenty as not. An' if He loved you, He would, too.'

"Of course I wasn't goin' to let he talk o' my Father like that, so I turned round 'pon en: 'Pray, Sir,' says I, 'who may you happen to be, comin' to me a-talkin' like this here? If I ben't mistaken, I know you, Sir; and I know my Father, too. And to think o' your comin' a-sayin' He don't love me! Why I've got your written character home to my house; and it do say, Sir, that you be a liar from the beginnin'. An' I'm sorry to add that I used to have a personal acquaintance with you some years since, and I served you faithful as ever any poor wretch could: and all you gave me was nothing but rags to my back, and a wretched home, and an achin' head,—an' no taturs,—and the fear o' hell-fire to finish up with. And here's my dear Father in heaven. I've been a poor servant of His, off and on, for thirty years. And He's given me a clean heart, and a soul full o' joy, and a lovely suit o' white as 'll never wear out; and He says that He will make a king of me before He've done, and that He'll take me home to His palace to reign with Him for ever and ever. And now *you* come up here a-talkin' like that.'

"Bless 'e, my dear friends, he went off in a minute, like as if he'd been shot—I *do* wish he had —and he never had the manners to say good mornin'."

A hearty laugh followed Dan'el's story. Even Widow Pascoe had to twitch her mouth into its propriety.

XII.

Dan'el's Notion of a Class-meeting.

I HAD dropt in to see Dan'el one evening before the service. It was in the late Autumn, and the days were "drawing in," so Dan'el looked up from his work with a smile of relief as well as of kindly greeting. He lifted the broad-rimmed spectacles on to his forehead, and laid down his work with the air of a man who could not do much more, and would enjoy half-an-hour's chat with a pleasant consciousness that he was not wasting his time.

It happened that just then local circumstances had directed attention to the Class-meeting. A correspondence in the papers was the talk of the uneventful month, rather because there was nothing else to talk of than because of any anxiety that was felt on the matter. It afforded a ready topic; so giving my old friend plenty of line, and encouraging him by a question here and there,—with which I need not break the narrative now,—I managed to get some notions that have not lost their value to-day.

"Class-meetin's be like awls and needles—they'll go so long as ever you can keep 'em bright; but when they get dull they'll rust, and then it be hard work. There was my old leader that I used to meet with, he was enough to kill any Class-meetin'.

"I was a young lad, so full o' joy as ever I could live, and my heart singin' to God all day long. And then I used to go up to Class, and it took all the music out o' me, like Granny's finery over the canary, and I couldn't do more than squeak a bit instead of singing at all. Why first of all he'd give out a hymn—one o' them for 'mourners'—like this,—

> 'Woe is me! what tongue can tell
> My sad afflicted state!
> Who my anguish can reveal,
> Or all my woes relate!'

And then they'd sing it to 'Josiah,' so slow as if

they was to a berrin'.* Or else it used to be that hymn—

> 'Ah! whither should I go,
>   Burden'd and sick and faint;
> To whom should I my troubles show,
>   And pour out my complaint!'

Then he had what he called a bit o' prayer. But there wasn't a bit o' prayer in it from beginnin' to end. It was all a groan about how bad we were, and what miserable sinners we were. He never thanked God for anything at all but this,—that He had not swept us away with the 'besom o' destruction.'

"And then he used to speak—it was all dismal an' mournin' about this 'howlin' wilderness,'—till I couldn't stand it any longer. I tried at first to feel so dull, and to speak so melancholy as he did. But it was no good my tryin'—not a bit. The Lord had put a new song into my mouth, and I couldn't help singin' it. So I thought I might as well speak out my mind about it, for all I was only a young lad. I can remember it quite well. 'Twas in the spring-time, and I'd been rejoicin' in all the beauty o' the world as I came along.

"'Well, my young brother, and how be you a-gettin' on?' he says, in his slow way.

"So I said, 'My dear leader, I don't know how it is, but I can't feel like you do, for the life o' me

---

* A funeral—at which hymns are frequently sung in Cornwall.

I can't. I don't feel any more like you do, than the day do feel like the night. Seemin' to me I *must* sing because my heart be so full. 'Tis like the spring down in the valley that be so full it must flow over. And if the Lord has made my heart to rejoice, I don't believe I ought to try and make myself feel any other. I've been and washed my robes and made 'em white in the blood o' the Lamb, and now I don't like to think that they are not white; it seem to me like insultin' my dear Lord for to go callin' 'em filthy rags. If my Lord has wrapt me up in the weddin' garment—and bless His dear Name He have!—it ben't right, and it ben't grateful, and it ben't true for me to go callin' 'em sackcloth and ashes. An' if I be drest for a weddin'—specially for the Marriage Supper o' the Lamb—I don't want to feel like as if I was a-goin' to a berrin'. I may be wrong, but I do think that the world be a brave deal more like God's world when the flowers be out, and the May be 'pon the hedges, an' the trees be all green and beautiful, an' the birds be a-singin' everywhere, than when it be all dead and shiverin' with the cold, an' the trees all stript naked, and liftin' up their arms to heaven, like as if they were askin' for pity. "Howlin' wilderness" it may be, till the Blessed Lord come to us; *then* the wilderness do begin to bud and blossom as the rose, and rejoice with joy an' singin'. And it says that " *the ransomed o' the Lord shall return, and come to Zion with* songs and everlastin' joy 'pon their heads: they shall obtain joy and gladness, and sorrow an' sighin' shall *flee away.*" Bless the Lord, my dear leader, I be His child! He has ransomed me, and now I can't help it—and I don't want to, neither—my heart be singin' all day long. I joy in Him by Whom I have now received the atonement. Why, I be a child of God, dear leader, an' I can't help walkin' about so happy as a king; for it be my Father's world, and there ben't a thing in it anywhere but is workin' together for my good. Bless the Lord, that's how I be gettin' along: it may be right, or it may be wrong, but that's 'zactly how it be.'

"I didn't mean to say so much, but I felt it, and when once I open my mouth it be hard work to shut en' again till it be all said. The old leader didn't like it. He turned quite red, and gave me a sly rap or two. But he wasn't a bad sort of a man, only a bit hasty in his temper for all he had so little fire in his bones. Before the week was over he went to the minister and told him that though I was so young he thought I might have a Class-book and get some members, for he was gettin' old, and couldn't do as he used to; and we two were all right after that. Nobody rejoiced more when I began to pick up a few members than he did.

"But talk about Class-meetin's, and people not comin to 'em: why the reason is pretty much the same as I was a-tellin' Bob Byles's wife the other day,—that it wasn't all his fault that he was home so little, and at the public-house so often. If she kept a bright fireplace, and a snug corner, and a pleasant smile for him at home, he would be tempted oftener to stay at home. We leaders must keep the place bright and cheerful and attractive if we want to keep the members. Why, I should every bit as soon think o' goin to Class with the wax an' the grease on my hands, as soon think o' goin' with my apron on and in my shirt sleeves, as think o' takin' all my cares and worries. I get away first of all and lose all my own fears and troubles in the lovin' care of my Heavenly Father. I get my own heart put into tune, and then the rest 'll take the right pitch from me. And then with the fire burnin' I get away to meetin'. We always begin with a good, cheerful hymn—one o' them that do stir up your soul, and a good old tune that you can sing without thinkin' about it, because you do know it so well. Give me a 'trumpet metre' to 'Arise my soul, arise!' or dear old 'Jerusalem,' to the hymn—

'My God, the spring of all my joys,
  The life of my delights,
The glory of my brightest days,
  And comfort of my nights!'

"Bless 'e, why, by the time you're gone through that, and had a bit o' downright earnest prayer, the fire is burnin' in every heart, and you're all aglow with holy joy. No fear o' freezing the tender lambs to death then: more likely to warm the old ones up to shoutin' pitch. When I hear some folks talk about the Class-meetin's as they do, I wonder whatever the leaders can have been about for to let 'em get such notions as they have got. I know faults are thick when the love is thin; and standin' water 'll breed plenty o' nasty things without anybody goin' nigh it. The old mill-wheel 'll creak and grumble when the river be low. But you can't wonder that folks don't like Class-meetin's if there be nothing for 'em when they do come: neither meat, nor drink, nor fire, nor a nice hearty welcome.

"I was down to the Infirmary the other day, and while I was waitin' there, they were all a-tellin' o' their ailin's and failin's. One had a cough, and another had a pain here and a weakness there, and another had a crushed hand, and another a bad eye. Now it didn't do 'em much good for to tell each other how bad they were. But directly the doctor come out. He never said a word about his own ailin's and failin's. But he looks in a cheerful kind o' way, and cheers up one, and has a pleasant word for another, and begins to examine another to see what be amiss with him, and tells him very serious that he must take care. And he writes down the medicines they want, an' tells 'em all to come next week.

"Now that be just what a leader ought to be,—a kind o' doctor that can give each one the prescription he needs—the blessed promise that suits his case; that can deal out the Lord's medicines, and can make up a strengthenin' plaster for them as is weak in the back and can't stand very well, and can clap up a stiff blister to them as have caught the fever o' worldliness, and can make a pill for sluggish *livers*—I do find that be the commonest kind of ailin'. That's what a leader ought to be,—a doctor who knows how to deal out the Lord's blessed cure-all, and can tell wounded consciences how to get whole, and them as is hard o' hearin' how they may hear the gentlest whisper o' that still small Voice, and can help dim eyes to get a clear, strong vision that can look on the glorious sun all day long; iss, and can see the Sun o' Righteousness in the middle o' the darkest night.

"But theare, nobody feels less fitted for it than I do; but I *can see* what it ought to be: I can see that much. And if everybody saw that, perhaps they would come a little bit nearer to doin' it and bein' it. A dinner o' herbs be better than some things; but the man who hasn't got anything else for the guests won't have much company, whatever name he may call it by. We shan't get folks very often to come into a *desert place* and rest awhile, if we, like the disciples, *forget to take bread.* If we want the folks to come we must have it now as it was then, and as it always will be when the Blessed Master be with us.—*They did all eat, and were filled. All*—nobody was forgotten. It was a big Class-meetin' that, but everybody got a bit: not an old woman was shut out by the crowd; not a hungry child was past by because it was afraid to ask; not a little maid but got a bit. That be just what I do want my Class-meetin' to be; a bit for all round—old and young, weak an' strong. A bit for everybody. And, bless the Lord, more than a bit too! '*They did* ALL *eat,*'—but that's only half of it, only the beginnin'—'*They did all eat and were filled.*'—FILLED. Ah! that's just like Him—*filled.* He don't give us a taste and leave us hungerin' for more. He 'SATISFIETH *thy mouth with good things.*' '*They did all eat, and were filled.*' Now that's a Class-meetin' 'zactly to my mind. And if we'll take the trouble to bake our bit o' bread, and catch our fishes, never mind though they be nothing but little sprats,—a few small fishes,—and if we'll put 'em into our Blessed Lord's hands, it'll be over again just what it was then—they shall all eat and be filled. And then they'll come again. Sure enough, they'll come again!"

XIII.

Dan'el's Notions about Searching the Scriptures.

THIS was a great point with Dan'el. To the younger members the question was put very often,—"Now, do 'e stick to the Scriptures? You won't do anything without that; and if you mind that, you won't get far wrong." Whenever a time of religious awakening brought a number of young people to the Class an evening was sure to be devoted to this subject. Our chapter has grouped together many of Dan'el's sayings on this subject, rather than given the talk of any one meeting.

DANIEL'S NOTIONS ABOUT SEARCHING THE SCRIPTURES. 113

"We shan't get on without it, friends, not a bit, and the prayer we need to put up, every one of us, is this: *Lord, teach us to read.* Why the Word is everything. And yet, seemin' to me, there's scores of folks who count themselves religious and yet they haven't a morsel o' conscience about this. To go without their bit o' prayer would make 'em uneasy and fidgetty all day long: they'd expect that something or other would go wrong. But as to searchin' the Scriptures—why you'll see them take the Book 'pon a Sunday afternoon, and turn it over very solemn and very serious, and presently they begin to nod their heads, and soon they're snorin' over the page. Good old John Bunyan, I'll warrant, had some of his neighbours in mind—he might have had some of mine—when he made Christian go to sleep whilst he was readin' the roll. Then they wake up, and count that that's enough to last for a week!

"No wonder so many go about cryin' 'My leanness, my leanness,' and are so weak that you can knock 'em down with a feather or trip 'em up with a straw. And a plague they are too. Talk about endurin' hardness as good soldiers! Why if poor brother Feeble-mind only gets a cap snapt at him, he flings up his work and goes grumblin' and mumblin' about it all the rest of his days; and if you happen to step on sister Ready-to-halt's toe she'll

I

limp for a year. For at best we are babes; but without searching the Scriptures we are babes without any milk—poor little frettin', pulin', wasted things.

"St. John says, '*I write unto you, young men, because ye are strong, and the Word of God abideth in you.*' 'Tis the man that 'meditates' in the law of the Lord that comes to be *like a tree planted;* you know 'em in a minute,—fixed, steady, immovable kind o' folks who don't mind a bit of a storm, and hold on though it blows great guns, as they say. But religious people who don't meditate in the law of the Lord, are commonly like the chaff —without any root, whirled about by their own feelin's; now whirled up into the third heaven, wonderful high up, a'most out o' sight; and now down again in the mud, trampled under foot. They meant well enough, but they didn't get hold o' the Word and stick to it, and so they had nothing to hold by, and it was all up and down with 'em, and in an' out, and in the end just nothing at all.

"There's hundreds o' young converts start fair enough, but they founder a'most before they're out o' the harbour, because they don't study the sailin' orders, and stick to the compass. They don't 'bide by the Word. The Blessed Master says in the New Testament just the same as David says in the Old. Buildin' on His sayings is buildin' on a rock. But buildin' on our own notions and feelin's and hopes and desires is poor stuff. The first bit of a breeze and a smart shower and 'tis all over with 'em. Backsliders are mostly made that way. They come in with the tide and they go out with the tide, for they don't heave out the anchor and hold on to the sure promise o' the word.

"The law of his God is in his heart; none of his steps shall slide" nodded young Cap'n Joe, as Dan'el paused a moment.

"Prayer is very good, and there's no gettin' on without that, but I don't believe prayer is prayer without the Word. Prayer is no good without faith, and faith cometh by the Word o' God. I know 'tis so with me. I can't pray right till I get hold of a promise; then I can go so bold as a lion. Why if I was to go down to Redburn and walk into the bank and ask for five pounds, they'd take me for a crazy man. What bis'ness have I got in there askin' like that? But when I go down there with a cheque for five pounds—or five hundred for that matter—I go straight in and I put it down and I pick up my money and come out again. Now that's just how I do dearly love to go up to the throne o' the heavenly grace. The Bible is a great book o' cheques and all you got to do is to put your name in. They're all signed, ready an' waitin'."

"Bless Him, they are all yea and amen in

Christ Jesus," whispered dear old Frankey in his corner.

"And then 'tis when a man is searchin' the Scriptures that he begins to see what he wants and what he ought to be. He sees the blessings he may have, an' it stirs up his desires and sets him a-longin' and hungerin', like when a hungry man is comin' home and he catches a sniff o' something savoury from a neighbour's door, it quickens his steps and sets him thinking' hard about his dinner. Prayer without the word is a heartless kind o' thing. There isn't any grip about it.

"There's two things wanted to get along in this religious life, and you won't do much with only one of 'em—The Bible and prayer; prayer and the Bible. We can't get along this river with only one oar in the boat—we shall only keep pullin' round and round. Scores and hundreds o' religious people are to-day just where they were ten, twenty, thirty years ago, 'zactly in the same place. They've got no more light, no more power, no fresh scenery; nothing altered. They say there's '*no standin' still in religion.*' Well then there's a deal o' lying still —that's all. Folks keep all their old tempers and ailin's and failin's just as if time had stood still; and the reason is that they've only one oar in the boat and they keep pullin' theirselves round an' round. We must have the other out too; we shan't do anything without it. We must get out the Word and begin to pull with it, and then, though it may be slow, we shall keep going on.

"To my mind that's just how 'tis that our fathers went ahead of us so much. They were mighty learned in the Scriptures, and didn't trouble their heads much about any other kind o' learnin'; and in spiritual power there were giants in those days! But now we go runnin' about increasin' knowledge. The newspapers come busyin' everybody about everything that's happenin' anywhere, and a man must know all that's going on in France and Russia and out in all them foreign parts. Nobody is ever took up for stealing a pair o' boots or trespassing after a hare but you must stop to read all about it; and all the time the Bible is kept under your finery as if it was much too good for every day; or else there's a great pile o' books 'pon top of it, like as if every kind o' reading come before that.

"The first thing I found out when I began to search the Scriptures was this,—that it isn't much good just *readin' the Bible*. The Word itself doesn't say anything that I can remember about readin' it. But it says a great deal about *searchin'* the Scriptures. And it says a great deal more about *meditatin'* on them. I have heard folks say—and they've been very sorry as they've said it—that they couldn't get any good in readin' the Bible. Any little bit of a story, or somebody's sermon, or a bit of any other religious book did 'em more good than this. They can't understand how David could have found it more precious than gold, and 'sweeter than honey.' Here's the reason,—they only read it, and David *meditated* in it.

"I don't know much about pearls, but I've heard tell that they come from the bottom o' the sea. Now we come up and look at the great stretch o' water, and say, 'This is where they get the pearls from;' and we take up the water, and get nothing but bubbles o' foam. 'Pooh,' we say, 'why that's not pearls!' and we go away wonderin' what people mean by talking as they do. But David comes along, and he dives down under the water, down ever so far, and he brings up a wonderful pearl, and so says he, It's '*more to be desired than gold, yea, than much fine gold.*' That's it. Readin' skims, and can't find anything but what floats along 'pon top; meditation dives down deep, and finds pearls.

"You know, one day the disciples heard our Lord's parable about the sower. They could make nothing of it: it was all strange and dark, and they couldn't see anything in it. That was just like 'tis to us when we read the Word sometimes. But when they got to a quiet place they said, '*Lord, declare unto us this parable.*' Then He began to explain it; and slowly it came before them all simple and beautiful, and did them all good. Now that is what we want: sittin' down in a quiet place askin' the Lord to explain it to us, and havin' our ears open to hear every word, and then it all comes so plain an' blessed, *'sweeter than honey and the honeycomb.'* Or just like the man that we read about in the Acts, who was ridin' along in his carriage, readin' the Bible, and he couldn't make anything of it. 'Who is the prophet talkin' about,' he says: 'is it about himself, or some other man.' Then Philip sat down alongside of him, and it came out all clear and beautiful, and he found the pearl of great price in the Word that seemed so hard to be understood,—he found Jesus, and believed with all his heart, and was baptized, and *'went on his way rejoicin'.'* Now readin' would ha' shut up the book and said, 'Dear me, I can't tell how folks get any good out of this here!' But meditation brings the Blessed Spirit to us, and He opens our eyes to see wondrous things out of His law, and we do begin to see the Blessed Lord, an' full o' joy and peace in believin' we go on our way rejoicin'.

"There's a blessin' in every bit of it, only we must get into it, and that's turnin' it over and meditatin' upon it. 'Tis like one o' them nuts with the milk inside. Here's a poor parched traveller, and he picks it up—'Call this delicious,' says he.

'or refreshin'! Why, it's nothing but husks and wood,' and he flings it away. And another thirsty wayfarer goes by. 'Here's a lucky find!' he cries out; and he strips off the husk, and bores into it, and gets a refreshin' draught. Meditatin' upon it we get in at the sweetness of it. That's why 'tis, my friends, that we can't get along with the Bible like David did. We *read* it; David *meditated* on it.

"And 'tis n't only for gettin' at the truth o' the Scriptures that we must turn it over in our thoughts like that. We want more than that. *We want to get the truth into us.* Folks read the Bible like a beggar looks into a baker's shop: he sees the rows of loaves, but he can't lay his hand on 'em. Only the difference is this, that the beggar has got an appetite if he could only get at one of 'em. We are so faint and so weak that we don't care to do any more than look. Now meditation is like gettin' the hand on the truth that feeds us. Samson didn't only look at the bees' nest, but he got at the honey and took it in his hands and went on eatin' it. 'Tisn't only seein' the truth but gettin' the truth into us. That's what David did. '*Thy Word have I hid in mine heart, that I might not sin against Thee.*'

"I've heard say that 'tisn't what we eat but what we digest that does us good. I know that's true in feedin' the soul. Why no kind o' thoughts are much to a man till they get into his heart. Passin' thoughts be like the bees that light for a moment and are off again before they can gather honey or leave a sting; they do neither good nor harm. But when a thought comes into a man's mind and begins to wake up the desires and stir the heart, then it does something; and you'll see what the man is like; for desires grow up into resolutions and it comes up in full-grown sayin's and doin's; and thoughts like that are the makin' of a man or the ruin of him. Now that's just where we must get the truth o' God's blessed Book. 'Tisn't much to read, but *then* we begin to feel it, and the strength and blessin' and peace of it goes all through us, and we get to be like the young men, strong because *the* Word abideth in us.'

"And, dear friends, in these times when life is all so busy and the soul has got such lots o' cares going rumblin' and rollin' over it, makin' it hard and barren like a highway, nothing but meditatin' on the truth will get it into us. When the fields are dried up with the heat they want more than the evenin' dew and a passin' shower. We want a kind o' a soakin' rain that don't run over the surface, but do get right down to the roots. And nothing else 'll do it for us but a quiet, steady meditatin' before the Lord 'pon His Word. Why I believe that if some o' the Lord's feeble folk would try this

—just a half-an-hour's quiet thinkin' over the Lord's Word—they'd hardly know theirselves in a month, and their nearest friends would begin to think that they were ripenin' for glory, sure 'nough.

"When a man begins the day like that he do keep such a glow of God's presence and favour about him, just like Moses came down from the Mount and went among the people, and his face shone still, go where he would. And then it do keep the mind all so fresh and clean and give a flavour to all the thoughts. It always minds me of when I was a little lad runnin' about the kitchen, and I've seen my mother pick a bay leaf and put in among the marinated pilchards. ''Tis'nt much,' she'd say, 'but it gives 'em a flavour, Dan'el; it gives 'em a flavour.' Ay, 'tis wonderful how a leaf o' the Tree o' Life will keep its sweetness and make all that it's put into sweet and nice! And then all day long it'll gather good thoughts about it, like the laurel tree home in my bit o' garden. There isn't any hive about here that I know of, but for all that the bees 'll be humming about there from sunrise to sunset. No, my dear friends, we shan't get along a bit without it, and we shan't go far wrong if we do stick to it. '*Search the Scriptures*,' says our Blessed Lord; '*they are they which testify of Me.*' But come, let somebody else tell us how they manage."

The sharp little eye peered across to young Cap'n Joe, confident that in this matter he could add something to what had been said. Nor had he to wait long.

"Well, my dear leader," Cap'n Joe began, "there is just one thing that I dare say you can manage better than some of us. You see, we can't always get that half hour's quiet. I'm sure we could get it very often when we don't care to; and a little bit off our sleep would go a long way to wake up our souls—I'm sure of that. But there are times when you can't get it anyhow. When there's anything amiss up to the mine, I'm there late at night, and have to be there early in the morning. Now how is a man to manage then?"

Many a head nodded its sympathy with Cap'n Joe.

"Manage, Cap'n," cried Dan'el, as a merry twinkle played about his eye, "why there's times as I can't stay to get my dinner sittin' down to it proper, but I don't starve for all that. I get a snack now and then, a bit here an' there, in the middle o' my work. 'Tis no reason why a man should starve because he can't sit down fitty to the table, and have a knife and fork and a table-cloth, and all the rest of it. Give me a pasty under a hedge with my old clasp-knife, and I can make a dinner fit for a king. If we've got the appetite we shall get a meal somehow. To begin with now, there be hours in a busy day when a man's head isn't taken up with anything though his hands have got to keep at it. And if he can put something good into his thoughts he can be turnin' it over, however busy he may be. When I've got to begin work early in the morning, I open my Bible at night, an' pick out a passage for the next day. As soon as I get up I look at the words and say them over to myself three or four times; then I shut up the Book and hurry away as fast as you like; for wherever I've got to go, or whatever I've got to do, I can keep thinkin' over the text, and kind o' inwardly digestin' it, as the prayer says. But you don't belong to the starvin' sort, Cap'n Joe—how do you manage now?"

Cap'n Joe's reply was in pulling out a little pocket Testament. "Just as you said, leader, if I can't have my dinner at home I carry it with me; and a man must be hard up if he can't find a place to eat it when he has got it in his pocket."

"Precisely, Cap'n. If we make up our minds to do it, we shall; and if we don't mind about it, we sha'n't. 'Tis with this like 'tis with everything else. But, Frankey, we must have a word from you. What's your opinion about this here matter?"

"Well, my dear leader, I don't know as my 'pinions be worth anything, but, bless the Lord, His

Word be everything to me—everything;" and a radiant joy spread over the wasted face, and every word trembled with deep emotion. " Whilst I've been sittin' here, I've been a-thinkin' about my boy over to Australia. He says how he do look out for a letter from home, and when it comes how he reads it over an' over. One day he was bad o' fever, and the man that he was along with waited 'pon him, and tended him, he said, like a mother; and just when the boy was gettin' better the man comes in and says, 'You won't want for medicine, now; here's a letter from home!' And the boy wrote back by next post to say that it cured 'en 'most directly.

"Dear lad, out there all alone to have word comin' that we do think about him, an' pray for him, and love him! And so I read my Father's letter and feel all His love and care for me, and know that home there to my Father's House they do think about me, and get a place ready for me, for all I'm nothing but poor old Frankey,—it be wonderful, wonderful, sure 'nough! And the boy, we can only send him a letter once a month, but seemin' to me as if I had a letter from my Father every day, and such wonderful letters too—bless His dear Name! Then sometimes we got wisht tidin's to send the lad; and it be all full o' poor speed; but there's nothing but good tidin's in my

Father's letters. Nobody is ever afeard to begin to read one o' em, thinkin' somethin' bad have happened, like we did when the boy couldn't write hisself, and the man had to write for 'en, and we turned all cold so soon as ever we see the strange writin'. Bless Him, His letters be always full o' rejoicin', and I do open 'em making sure that everything be right; for nothing can '*separate us from the love of God, which is in Christ Jesus our Lord.*'

"The dear boy says that when he begins to read the letter 'tis like as if he was home again, and he can see us all, and do know just what we're all a-doin' of. And that's how 'tis sometimes when I'm readin' the Word; instead of bein' only words wrote down in a book, 'tis all livin' and real, and I can see it all and feel it all. It minds me always of the prophet when he stretched hisself out 'pon the dead child, and the child began to get warm, and opened his eyes and spoke out. It be wonderful, wonderful, how we can stretch ourselves out 'pon the promises—lie down on 'em full length,—and they begin to live, and speak, and ben't words that somebody spoke a long time ago, but do come fresh and warm from the lips o' the Blessed Lord, all full o' His gentle love and tenderness an' power. O, my dear leader, the Word is everything! And I was thinkin' how I should love to write a letter out to the dear boy, sayin', 'Come home, for we can live home here now, all of us, and I'm quite well, and we sha'n't want any more, but we'll be all together so happy as we can live.' Ah, bless Him, that is how I sometimes read it in my Father's letters. It won't be long—I expect it every post now, the message that'll say: '*Rise up, My love, and come away.*'"

XIV.

On Two Ways to Heaven.

I USED to think that there was only one way to heaven.

"I know now that there's two. There's only one gate to go in at, and they both lead up to the one golden gate at the other end; but there's two paths from one to the other.

"'Tis just like the fields goin' up to Brea. You get in over the stile, and as soon as you're over there's two footpaths, and you may go along which you've got a mind to. One is down by the side o' the ditch, all in between furze bushes, an' there's some ugly old shafts about there covered over with nothing but bramble bushes, an' there's nothin' to see but a great stone wall all along. The other way is up higher: 'tis a bit of a climb at first: but you get up above the furze bushes, and then you have a good view all round and a draught o' fresh air, an' you can look out 'pon the blue sea and the glorious white clouds risin' up ever so far off, like a land where there's no sin. Now seemin' to me that's just like some folks goin' to heaven. Good folks, I'm sure, an' they've come in the right way an' they'll get to heaven if they keep on; but they're all among the furze bushes, an' old tangled ways, draggin' theirselves through brambles an' brakes; they've got to keep lookin' for the right way, an' they can't see anything of the view for the great stone hedge. However it may come about, so it is. Some folks 'll find a way to heaven that'll keep 'em singing all along, so happy as a lark. They serve the Lord with gladness. But other folks 'll go sighin' an' fearin' an' worryin', and always be in a way chuck-full o' brambles an' furze bushes.

"I don't believe you can explain it, by talkin' about what some have got to bear, an' what some have got to do without; some pilgrims goin' along the way bare-foot, an' some goin', as folks say, in silver slippers. That won't account for it; I've met Bare-foot many a time runnin' along like a strong man in the upper path, and I've seen

K

Silver-slipper and gouty Prosperity go limpin' along the lower way. Look at dear old Frankey—bless him, I'm 'fraid we sha'n't have him with us much longer! Now if any of us is goin' to heaven bare-foot, that's Frankey; and yet he's 'pon the mountain-top all day long. I've just come from seein' him, and what he said has set me a thinkin' about this matter. His cough was bad, sure 'nough, but his face was lighted up with glory.

"'Just outside o' the golden gates, I reckon, Frankey?' I says to him.

"''Iss, my dear leader, just outside. I can 'most hear their music.'

"'But seemin' to me that you've been 'pon the steps for years a'ready, Frankey.'

"'Well, is'nt it the best place to get to?' he said, between his breath. 'If Lazarus could come an' lay hisself down at the rich man's gate an' pick up the crumbs from the rich man's table, why he'd ha' been a stupid to ha' stayed away an' starved—would'nt he? And I soon found out that my dear Lord did'n' mean me to go about so miserable as I could be, but that I might come right up to the golden gate o' my Father's house, where, bless Him, there's bread enough an' to spare; an' that I might pick up the crumbs o' heaven's glory, so much as ever I could carry. It would be strange if I'd stayed away an' perished of hunger? Why, I should ha' been a stupid, shouldn't I, my dear leader?'

"'Strange, 'iss Frankey, 'twould,' I said; 'an' 'tis wonderful how many o' the pilgrims goin' to heaven be strange, sure 'nough—stranger here than they'd be in anything else. Walkin' when they could ride, and ridin' third-class when they could go first just as cheap.'

"'Ridin'! my dear leader,' says Frankey, lookin' so happy: 'why bless 'e 'tis more like flyin' home, flyin' up like a lark, an' you can't help singin' as you go.'

"Now friends, I've been thinkin' as I came along here that this is a secret worth tryin' to find out. I've thought about it very often before now. Once when I was up to London I was goin' to the Crystal Palace, and I asked a policeman to show me where to get my ticket.

"'There's two lines,' he said; 'which do you want?'

"Of course I told him I wanted the best, an' asked what difference there was between them.

"'Well,' said he, 'they both start from this station, an' they both get to the Palace. They call one the *high-level*, and the other the *low-level*. One runs right into the Palace, and there you are. The other sets you down not far off, only you've got to go up scores o' stairs before you're into the place itself.'

K 2

"'Ah,' I says in a moment, 'if that's it, give me the *high-level o' course.*' An' I wondered that anybody ever went the other way.

"That set me a meditatin' about it. Folks goin' to heaven by the low level; goin' down under their privileges; goin' to heaven, but ever so much lower than they might be; goin' through tunnels an' cuttin's, instead o' bein' up in the light an' sunshine a-viewin' the landscape o'er. And then when the journey's done, seemin' to me they'll have a great lot o' stairs to climb up somehow.

"I fancy sometimes that I can see the beginnin' of it. You start from the same station, but the lines are different. There's Paul startin' for the celestial city—I was goin' to say the Crystal Palace, and it wouldn' have mattered much if I had, for it is that. Paul got right off 'pon the high level at the very first. He says, '*Lord, what wilt Thou have me to do?*' It was *Thou*. He hadn' a great big capital I stuck in his thoughts, so big that he couldn' see anything else. But the jailer cried out —'*What must I do to be saved?*' It was I, all I with him. Of course he was only a heathen, and p'raps came to see different after they'd spoken the word o' the Lord to him. But whatever he did, there's thousands o' people who never get beyond that. '*What must I do to be saved?*' It is all this great I. They hug it, and love it, and bring it up to be saved. Mind you, I don't say that it isn't right. '*What shall a man give in exchange for his soul?*' We are every one of us bound to make our callin' an' election sure. A man comes to Jesus seekin' his own salvation, like this, an' he shall find it too; and if he holds on he shall get to heaven. But for all that 'tis the *low-level*. And Paul went along a more excellent way. The high-level starts there where a man doesn't see hisself so much as he sees his Blessed Lord, and he sees what his sins have done,—and he hates himself, for he sees how he has injured an' grieved an' hurt his Lord; and he sees his Blessed Saviour as the '*altogether lovely*'—and he falls down at His feet, and wants to do anything for Him. All his soul cries out—'*Lord, what wilt Thou have me to do?*'

"That's how the ways begin. And that's how they go on. The Low-level man climbs over the stile, and he sees the path that goes down the hill. Thinkin' all about hisself, he says: 'Well, I'll save myself this bit of a climb,' an' so he gets down among the brambles an' brakes. An' ten to one but he'll go sighin' an' grumblin' and thinkin' what a hard road it is to travel, this **road** to Zion; and when he gets to Class he'll have nothin' to talk about but his temptations an' troubles—and the worldly folks that are over the other side, will say—*What a dismal thing religion is!* But the High-level man jumps over the stile to meet his Blessed Lord. When he sees the path goin' up the hill-side, he says, 'Why I shall be nearer to Him up there, and shall see more o' His beauty.' He climbs up the stiff bit, and then he goes singin' along in the sunshine, with a lovely view. Poor *Low-level* is goin' to the same place, but he'll see nothing but a great stone wall, and the worst of it is that he'll have to climb twice as much when he gets to the other end o' the field.

"There's scores o' people goin' on like that. They are very religious, but their religion has never got into the sunshine and the joy. And the reason is just this—that *they only think about theirselves.* They pray, but 'tis only that the Lord would take care o' them, and feed 'em and clothe 'em, and bring 'em safe home at last. But on the *high-level* a man doesn't care so much to ask for anything as to get into the presence of his dear Lord, and feel how good an' kind He is, an' then try all day to please Him. *Low-level* keeps a-sayin', 'I hope the Lord'll keep me to the end.' *High-level* keeps a-sayin', '*My meat an' my drink is to do the will of my Father which is in heaven.*'

"The Psalmist says, '*Serve the Lord with gladness.*' But *Low-level* doesn't think about servin' the Lord, so much as *the Lord servin' him.* Or if he does set hisself for to serve the Lord, 'tis for a crown an' a robe by way o' wages. Trust 'em, they won't forget theirselves. There's gladness for anybody when they'll set theirselves with all their heart to please their dear Lord, and keep on doin' it. That love 'll take 'em right up to the throne—right up alongside o' the angels an' archangels who serve Him day and night in His temple.

"Why when I was a little lad there were some days, that I can mind now like as if it was only yesterday. The sky was such a wonderful bright blue, and the flowers were all such a wonderful colour, and the birds a-singin', too, wonderful, and everything I saw an' heard was so full o' strange beauty and a kind o' delicious joy, that I had to dance with very gladness. Ah, I can mind quite well how it was. 'Twas when I set myself to please my mother, and tried to do it all day long, and did it too; an' she'd see me tryin', and used to give me a smile or a word o' love. Eh, talk about heaven; about what is there, and what isn't there. I don't care so much about that. That's heaven down here and up above too—when a man has set himself to please the Lord, and He whispers to his heart, 'Well done, good servant.' Why if 'tis in a tumble-down cottage, or a mighty palace, 'tis all one: that man enters into the joy of his Lord. That's heaven.

"No wonder poor Low-level is so dull—the only

wonder would be if he were anything else. He carries *himself* about with him like a great pair o' blinkers that shut out the view and shut him up in the dark. But *High-level* gets up on the top o' the delectable mountains an' gets out his spy-glass, and forgets himself, because he sees so much o' the love an' wisdom an' power an' glory of his Blessed Lord; and he begins to praise Him with all his heart, because he can't help it. How can he do anything else but praise Him when he sees how good an' kind an' wise He is? And how can anybody be any other than dismal and dull when he keeps his thoughts always 'pon his own self? He'll have to look a long time before he sees much to sing about there. If we don't want dull thoughts to come we must keep 'em away like I keep the weeds out o' my bit o' garden. I fill the bed so full o' flowers that there isn't any room for weeds. Let a man live where he can keep his mind stayed 'pon his Lord, and he won't have much room for dismal old thoughts and fears about his own self.

> 'The op'ning heavens around me shine,
>   With beams of sacred bliss,
> If Jesus shows His mercy mine,
>   And whispers I am His.'

"Depend 'pon it 'tis just like this here: if we come to the Father only for what we can get, askin' for the portion o' goods, well, we shall have it because we are sons. But we shall always want something else. We shall never feel so full o' satisfaction that it'll have to run over into a bit o' singin', like the brook up to Carwinnin. 'Tis when we come to feel that the portion o' goods is very little—nothin' at all in comparison—but that the Father is everything, then our hearts begin to sing. Why, with the Father's blessed voice in our ears, and His arms about our necks, an' His love in our hearts, we can't help ourselves—we *must* begin to be merry.

"Paul went along *the high-level* because he died to his own self, and lived only for Christ. Pain and loss and trouble and death were nothing to Paul if he could only serve his Blessed Lord. But folks that go along *the low-level* are always wantin' the Lord to wait 'pon them with health and prosperity, sunshine an' best robes. I do dearly love to read an' think about Paul and his way to heaven. Why, my dear friends, we should hardly know ourselves if we went to live up there where Paul lived. I've heard folks who've come home from California say that out there the air is so pure that you can see miles an' miles, everything is so clear; and 'tis all so still that you can hear singin' miles off, an' 'tis always like summer over there, so that the bees' don't lay up any honey because there's no winter and no need for it. Now that's *the high-level* to heaven, 'zactly. 'Tis up where you can see ever so far, where you can always catch sight o' the golden gates, an' see the shinin' o' the Father's House, and when 'tis very still you can a'most hear the singin' inside. I wonder we don't emigrate right off to once, 'tis such a pretty country, an' no rates nor taxes. And like the bees, you've got honey up there all the year round, no great black clouds o' care comin' about like a hurricane, and no ugly old fears keep a whisperin' about the winter, an' whatever we shall do to get along then. Why 'tis down here for us as well as up there, if we would only have it:—

> 'There everlasting Spring abides
> And never-withering flowers.'

And if you like to ask why we don't live there, the answer is plain enough,

> '*Self*, like a narrow sea, divides
> This heavenly land from ours.'

"Seemin' to me that Paul made short work of self. He gave self notice to quit, an' gave up the freehold to his Blessed Lord. And I mean to try and follow his example and to say to my own self, 'Dan'el I won't have you for a tenant any longer: you're more trouble to me than all the world besides. You're so hard to please, an' so uncertain that if you happen to be all right to-day, there's no knowin' what you'll be like to-morrow. I shall turn 'e out, neck an' crop with all your goods and chattels.' That's what I want for my own self, friends. My heart cries out, 'My Lord, come in and live in this house, not like a great visitor for me to entertain, and ask a favour of now and then; but come in an' be the Master and I'll be the servant, an' all I am shall wait upon Thee.' That's what I want for myself; and then when anybody knocked to the door an' said—'Dan'el Quorm live here,—does he?' I should dearly love to say, Dan'el's gone away and he's dead an' buried: '*Nevertheless I live; yet not I, but Christ liveth in* me.'

"Paul gives us a good many short cuts across from *the low-level* to *the high*. There's one in the twelfth chapter o' Romans and in the first verse. '*I beseech you, brethren, by the mercies of God, that ye present your bodies a livin' sacrifice, holy, acceptable unto God, which is your reasonable service.*' Now, seemin' to me, that's plain enough for anybody. Here's the house, a three-storeyed house, consistin' o' body, soul and spirit. You go on month after month, an' year after year, sayin' what you'd like to do an' what you mean to do. I've heard scores o' sermons about this text, an' heard it talked about hundreds o' times, and I've heard folks say in their prayers that they desired to do it. But hearin' about it, an' talkin' about it, and prayin' about it, like that isn't a morsel o' good. Here, take the key, and go right away and give it up to the Lord once for all, and have done with it. We go dilly-dallying about it year after year, till the old walls fall in and there's nothing left but a heap o' rubbish. '*Present your bodies,*' says Paul. Go in before the Lord, and say here I am, Lord take me, altogether, Thine and Thine for evermore. Give Him the house an' let us just sweep the rooms an' keep it so nice as ever we can for Him. The Lord help us, every one, to be *high-level* Christians."

So Dan'el finished, and a hearty Amen came from most of the members. For a moment there was silence, for Dan'el often broke through the set form and routine of speaking, and encouraged a conversation. Then it was that young Cap'n Joe struck in.

"Well, friends, I don't know how 'tis with you, but there isn't a subject in the world that has been more in my thoughts lately than this that our leader has been talking about; only it seems to me as if he thought the bit of a climb was just nothing at all, and that a man could be up on *the high-level* in a minute. You talk about it as a path in a field, but to me 'tis something very different from that. I was down to Portreath the other day when the tide was out, and as I was walking along on the pier, I saw an old friend of mine on the sands below me. I leaned over and said in a joke,— 'Come up here!' he looked up; it was only twenty feet or so above him, 'Ah, I wish I could,' he said. It was twenty feet of granite wall without a foothold in it, and he had to go back a long way over the sands before he could get up. Now what you call a path in a field, is a good deal more like the face of a granite wall to me. I've tried to climb it till I'm ready to give up in despair, and sometimes it quite frets and vexes me to hear people talkin' about it as they do, for I've tried ever so hard, and never seemed to me to be so far away as I am to-night, for all my trying."

It was plain that young Cap'n Joe had hit a difficulty that was shared by many. Eyes met each other, and heads nodded in sympathy, and earnest faces were thrust forward to catch the reply.

A happy smile came over Dan'el's rugged face as he began:—"Ah, Cap'n Joe, I'm glad to hear what thou hast said. I'm fine an' glad that thou'st got so far as that. We've got to learn that lesson a'most before every step in religion—that we can't get on a bit in our own strength, but that 'tis accordin' to our faith. Why now, didn't you come to Jesus years ago as a poor sinner with the great burden 'pon your back? You wanted to get rid of it. How you tried to, till your fingers were a'most worn away, and you hadn't got any strength left. And when you couldn't do anything else, you came an' cast yourself 'pon the Blessed Saviour, an' prayed Him to do it all for you. Then when you trusted Him like that, your load fell off, and you wondered you hadn't come to Him long, long before. And so 'tis again here, dear friends. We want to be saved clean out of our sins, an' right out of our failins' an right up out of our ownselves. Well, we been tryin' to do it, and we can't; and now shall we give it all up in despair? No, no, we won't let the devil get the upper hand of us like that there. We do every one of us know too much about the dear Lord to do that. Come, we'll cast ourselves 'pon Him, an' take Him as all that our hearts are a-longin' after. Our Saviour from all sins; our Saviour from *sinnin'*; from our weaknesses an' hindrances an' failin's; accordin' to our faith it shall be to us again, just like 'twas at first.

"I picked up a lesson down to Redburn t'other day that I shan't forget in a hurry; 'twas back in the winter. They had a soup-kitchen, you know, down there. An' one day when I was comin' along I saw them comin' for their soup. There was the boys and girls with their mugs and their jugs; and, in amongst them came up an old grandmother who looked as if she'd plenty o' little hungry mouths at home, an' she brought a great big pitcher. I waited to see her come out again. The mugs were filled, and the jugs were filled; so I says to myself, 'I wonder if she'll get her pitcher full.' Yes there it was full to the brim, as much as she could carry with both hands. So I came home thinkin' about it. ' 'Tis a lesson for thee, Dan'el,' I says. ' Why thou'rt old enough to learn it too. Thou hast gone up to thy Lord's storehouse with a mug, and thou mightest ha' gone with a jug. A jug? 'iss, thou might'st ha' gone with a pitcher an' it would ha' been full. An' a pitcher needn't ha' been all. If thou wilt go with a faith so big as a horse an' cart thou shalt have as much as thou can'st carry.' Come, my friends, let us have a bigger faith, so big that it shall come to take the Blessed Lord as our All in all, fillin' all the heart an' all the mind, an' all the house. 'Tis too hard for us—but according to our faith it shall be unto us."

XV.

On Winning Souls.

STRANGELY enough, it was Widow Pascoe who most commonly suggested this topic. Partly by the selfishness of her sentiments, partly by her dismal looks and tones, but still more by the impression that all about her made on one's mind. Though she never said it in so many words, there were a hundred things about her that kept saying it over and over again—"The Lord's people are a *peculiar* people, a *little* flock. You only know that the way leads to Heaven if a very few there be that find it. Therefore receive all new comers with cold suspicion. Most likely they are hypocrites, and if not, they will probably be back in the world again in a month. Keep the way as much as you possibly can to yourself."

In her thinking, the road to Heaven was not only as gloomy and uncomfortable as you could make it, but it was walled up like the cities of Anak; and plenty of broken glass on the top of the walls would have been a real consolation to her mind. She would have had the entrance gate covered with spikes, and surrounded with notices of spring-guns and man-traps, and warnings that trespassers would be prosecuted with the utmost rigour of the law. As for "the grave and beautiful Damsel, named Discretion," whom Pilgrim found at the gate, Widow Pascoe would have given that fair maiden "notice," and have improved matters very much, in her own estimation, by installing herself as doorkeeper. Dan'el was constantly provoked by it into plain speaking, and nobody else in the Class had a particle of sympathy with a nature so ice-bound and narrow. But *that* was Widow Pascoe's comfort. To be misunderstood, to find that nobody agreed with her, to have no encouragement and no sympathy, was

L.

"a good time" to Widow Pascoe; all this was the most satisfactory evidence of her religion. It was meal-time to her when she could come hither and dip her parched corn in the vinegar—then she did eat, and was sufficed, and left.

Dan'el listened with a sigh, and spoke slowly and sadly,—" Well, if we don't take care, I'm 'fraid some of us'll never get to Heaven."

This was threatening: it even disturbed Widow Pascoe's composure for a moment.

Dan'el continued, as if explaining what had gone before,—" Or if we get there it won't be like the Lord Jesus went. You remember that Jesus wouldn't go to Heaven alone, even He took a soul with Him, and said: '*To-day shalt thou be with me in Paradise.*' An' the only safe way for us is to go like the Blessed Master went."

Another pause followed, in which the little eye regained its humorous expression, and a ripple of playful roguishness came over Dan'el's face.

" You know, my dear sister, you'll never get anybody to go along such a dismal old road as you make of it, never. An' what'll you do if you get up to the golden gate all by yourself? You know the Lord wouldn't let the beasts go into the ark one by one—not even the unclean beasts; not a cat or a dog could go in by itself. An' if 'tis anything like that, what will folks do who've never got a soul to go to Heaven with 'em. Besides, it would be a'most impudence to knock to the door an' ask the glorious great Archangel to open it just to let in one. When I was up to E—— once, I went in to see the Cathedral; and the man came up with a bunch o' big keys, and says he, 'You must wait a bit till somebody else come, for we don't show it to less than two at a time—it ben't worth while.' An' then when there was two of us, he opened all the doors, an' took us upon top o' the tower, and showed us about everywhere. Now seemin' to me 'twould serve us 'zactly right if we was to go up an' knock to the golden gate o' the celestial City, and the Archangel was to say, 'You should ha' found somebody else to come in with 'e,'—an' if he was to keep us waitin' outside till somebody else come up.

"An' it isn't a matter that we can please ourselves about either. The Lord Jesus tells us that we are *the lights of the world*, an' if that do mean anything at all, it do mean that somewhere somebody in the world is bein' cheered an' guided and helped to see things out there in the dark, by what we are a doin' of, or by how we are livin'. And the Lord tells us that we are *the salt o' the earth*. An' if we are not helpin' to keep some soul sweet an' clean, an' to preserve it unto everlastin' life, why I can't see much difference between that an' salt that has lost its savour: one doesn't do any good, and the other is good for nothing. And like everything else in God's world that is good for nothing, it shall be cast forth and '*trodden under foot.*'

"Why I meet lots o' the Lord's people who think it don't matter a bit how they let their lights shine, so long as they shine somehow. Some of 'em 'll flash it out and frighten anybody with it, like the glare of a policeman's bull's eye. I can mind an old gentleman who used to come to see my father: he'd take hold o' me by the collar o' my coat an' frown at me, an' say in a great gruff voice, 'Now be a good boy and do what you're told, or you'll go to the devil.' That never did me any good; I don't believe it would do anybody any good. And then there are others of 'em—why you might think they had to pay for it, an' was always afeared o' wastin' the gas. They'll turn it up 'pon a Sunday an' 'pon the prayer-meetin' night, an' they'll have ever so big a glare then; but so soon as ever they do get home, they'll turn it down so low that the children an' the neighbours think it be gone out altogether. Now seemin' to me the only kind o' light that'll do the world any good is a *burnin'* light—'a burnin' an' a shinin' light.' Some folks be like glow-worms, that shine without burnin'; but *they* won't do much good. We must *burn*, friends, *burn* an' then we shall shine. Let's long to win souls, an' feel the longin' burnin' in us, an' then we shall do it. Only let our hearts catch fire, then the world 'll see the light an' feel the warmth, an' some poor perishin' mortal or other 'll be sure to come up to get a bit o' life. But if we don't burn, we shan't shine much. That be the only kind o' light that's worth anything, 'a *burnin*' and a shinin' light.'

"An' the beauty of it is that every one of us can do it, whether we got one talent or whether we got two. Furze bushes and brambles ben't no good for buildin' o' the Lord's House,—you must have great cedars o' Lebanon for that,—nor yet for a makin' the furniture out of; but set 'em a fire, an' they 'll light up the country for miles an' miles. Never mind though you be reckoned nothin' in God's world but weeds an' rubbish, you can burn so as to give light in the dark. Dear old granny here can't do much, but 'pon a dark night she can begin to think about the folks that have got to come across the moors, an' that may be strayin' away an' gettin' down some old shaft or other; an' she can tell 'em to sweep up the hearth an' get a nice bright fire an' to pull up the blind, and let the candle shine right out 'pon the road. Somebody 'll be guided a bit, and get a bit o' warmth an' cheerfulness out there in the dark. An' I often think about it when I rake out my fire just afore goin' to bed. This here fire do burn away like that, and come to nothing but ashes; but they that begin to burn an' shine, tryin' to '*turn many to righteousness*,' shall never go out—they shall shine like '*the stars for ever and ever.*' 'Tisn't enough to be called the light o' the world an' the salt o' the earth, my friends. We must set about it the right way to do it. Folks may be the salt o' the earth: but they won't do much good if they come to you with a great mouthful of it that'll be a sickener for many a day, an' perhaps spoil your relish for it altogether. There's lots o' people who want to save souls, but 'tis '*they that be wise*' that '*shall shine as the brightness of the firmament.*'

"Now seemin' to me that the first thing *is to set ourselves to do it.* 'Tis just like everything else,—it wants doin'. It won't do it to be always talkin' about it, an' desirin' it, an' prayin' that we may be useful. We must get up an' do it. Simon said, '*I go a-fishin'.*' And he might have talked about it, and prayed about it all his life,—he never would have caught anything till he went. We keep sayin', 'Dear brethren, let us go a-fishin';' or, 'You know we really must go a-fishin'.' We talk of how very right an' proper it is, an' how we desire to do it, an' we go prayin' that we may be stirred up to go a-fishin'. But Simon gets out his bait-box, an' his cross-lines, an' he shoulders the oars an' he shoves off the boat, an' settlin' down he calls out to the rest of 'em, '*I go a-fishin'*. Then the rest, who perhaps had been talkin' about it, shoved off their boats too, an' said, '*We also go with thee.*' An' that's the way in fishin' for souls, you must set about it. Why we stand in on the shore loungin' about the quay with our hands in our pockets, thinkin' that if the fish are to be caught the Lord will send 'em to us. If we want them, we must *go a-fishing.*

"And then there's another thing I like about Simon—*he didn't mind goin' alone.* I'm 'fraid a good many of us would have seen Simon goin' out in his boat, an' never have said what the rest did. We should have kept our hands in our pockets, and have said, 'Quite right an' proper: he's called to the work;' or we should have said, 'O, he's a leader; he ought to go!'—or we should have said—'There goes Simon again: what a gift he has got for it!' Pack o' stuff an' nonsense. A gift for it! Why he had a hook an' a line an' a bit o' bait; and so he went out to do what he could. That was his gift for it, and that was his callin' too. I want for every one of us to say, '*I go.*'

"I was down to St. Ives once when the pilchards was about, and the man that was on the look-out up on top o' the cliffs saw the school of pilchards a-rufflin' the water, so he puts up a great speakin' trumpet to his mouth, and holloas out so loud as ever he could, '*Heva, heva, heva.*' All the people knew what he meant, and the place was all in a stir in a minute. The big boats put up sail, and went out to shoot their nets; and then when they'd got 'em all shut in everybody got in a boat and pulled out to lend a hand, an' the water was all covered with boats. Everybody went a-fishing' then. Now that's just like 'tis when the Lord sends a great revival, and everybody wakes up an' goes a-fishin'. But, la! my friends, there be fish in the sea all the year round. There's souls to be caught all the year round: summer an' winter; hot or cold; rain or fine. 'Tis never too rough to put your boat off to catch souls, an' 'tis never too calm. Don't let us wait till we can go out with the great nets; we can always go hookin'—catchin' 'em one by one. Every one of us can catch a soul here an' there, if we'll only try. I do dearly love that '*I go:*' like as if he said, 'You others may please yourselves, but as for me, I'm off.'

"There's something about Andrew too that is almost as good as what Peter said. '*He first findeth his own brother Simon.*' Now I'm sure that 'tis a good plan to go looking after one soul. Anything is fair play, I do count, 'pon the devil's ground.

Every soul in the world do belong to our Lord. He made 'em every one, and He bought 'em every one with His precious blood. They're His every way; and the devil is a thief. I've very often thought o' what a poor master the devil's servants have got. Why, when he come up to tempt our mother Eve in Paradise, he hadn't got any bit o' a little thing for to bribe her with, an' all he could do was to tempt her to steal her Master's apples. He haven't got anything at all of his own, an' I am sure he ha'n't got any souls belongin' to him. So I think 'tis quite fair to go catchin' souls any way you've got a mind to, an' whichever way you can. He isn't so very partic'lar about it, his own self: he's always a-comin' up poachin' 'pon our preserves, so bold as a lion; an' I don't see why we should mind how we can get back the souls that he has stolen, so long as we can get 'em back somehow.

"I can mind when I was a boy seein' the big folks come up to Carwinnin' with their fine rods an' lines an' wonderful turn out, an' they'd go all day an' never catch a fish. But we boys would see a fish go dartin' in under a stone: then we should get in an' go gropin' round the stone an' catch 'em like that. Well, I b'lieve in gropin' for souls. And seemin' to me that Andrew did too. He didn't say 'I'll try to do all the good I can,' and then do nothing because he couldn' find any to do. But he says,—'There's Simon. I'll go an' catch him.' That's the way. Pick out one soul, an' set your heart 'pon it,—begin to pray for that one an' try to catch that one, an' go on tryin' till you've got it; an' then try for another. We might do a good deal o' good in the world, if we didn't try to do so much. I've heard folks a-singing'—an' meanin' it too—

> 'Were the whole realm of nature mine,
> That were a present far too small;'

an' because the 'realm o' nature' wasn't theirs, they didn' give anything at all. But if they said, 'I've got five-an'-twenty shillin' a week; how much can I manage to screw out o' that,' then they'd have done something. An' that's the way with folks who want to go catchin' souls. They'll sing—

> 'O that the world might taste and see
> The riches of His grace!'

they want to convert the world, but because they can't do that, they won't try to save their next door neighbour.

"Now all that's cured if we'll just pick out one soul an' try to catch that. Let us do it, my friends. Let us begin this very day. There's somebody in your family, or there's a neighbour o' yours, or there's somebody that works up to your mine, or there' somebody that you often meet with goin' along your road. Pick out that one, an' say— 'Now, the Lord helpin' me, I'll try an' catch that there soul.' Pray that the Lord 'll give you a chance o' gettin' at 'em, an' keep on prayin': an' when you get the chance make a down-right good use of it. There isn't a door in this world but prayer 'll batter it down, if you keep hard at it. Bolts an' bars haven't got a chance against prayer. It can pick a lock that a London sharper couldn't do nothing with. Great gates an' draw-bridges, like them down to Pendennis Castle, can't help theirselves against it. Only pray in downright earnest, an' the door 'll open before long, an' then, when 'tis open, go in an' take possession in the name o' the King of kings. Depend 'pon it, that's how the world has got to be converted. Everybody who loves the Lord Jesus Christ must try, for His sake, to win somebody else, and must stick to it till they do.

"Then there's just one thing more about this catchin' souls. *'Tis a'most so good for ourselves as 'tis for those we try to save.* There's nothing else, I believe, that 'll make a man so watchful an' so careful about all he says an' does, as this will. When I used to go fishin' with a rod and line an' caught sight of a big fish under the bank, why I could keep so still as a mouse for half a day. Other times we might run about on the bank, an' jump about so much as we liked. But now a shadow mustn't fall 'pon the water; there mustn't be a sound; only just lettin' the bait drop in, so gentle and quiet. Ah, you go an' try to catch a soul if you want to be watchful! No hasty words then; that would scare the soul away in a minute. No bit o' quick temper or angry ways; that would spoil it all.

"Pick out your soul, an' begin to pray for it; set to work to catch it, an' we shall do it. Only set to work the right way. It isn't those who try, but those who try the right way—*the wise*—that shall shine as the stars. An' as for wisdom, for all it is the rarest thing in the world, bless the Lord we can get so much of it as ever we mind to, and all for nothing. 'If any of you;' never mind how dull a scholar he is, or how big a fool; '*if* ANY OF YOU *lack wisdom, let him ask of God, that giveth to all men liberally, and upbraideth not; and it shall be given him.*' So let us all say as Simon did, an' mean it too, by the Lord's help, *I go a-fishin'.*"

XVI.

On Hearing the Word.

'VE heard folks say — 'The child's the father o' the man,'—and there's more truth in that than there is in a good many things that folks say. Now I've been a-thinkin' that Sunday is the father o' the week -the rest o' the week 'll take after the Sunday, an' if anybody wants to have a good week let 'em try to get a good Sunday.

"I don't know how 'tis with you, friends, but I'm just like the old clock that's home to my place —I'm a sort o' machine that wants windin' up once a week, an' if I don't get wound up 'pon a Sunday I'm run down all the week. I've seen the farmers down to Redburn 'pon the market day pullin' out their watches an' settin' 'em by the old church clock, turnin' the hands a bit forwarder or a bit backwarder. But it isn't a bit o' good settin' 'em right if they forget to wind 'em up. Now I believe there's lots o' folks that'll come to the House of God 'pon a Sunday an' they'll set their feelings right; they'll get very nice and religious for a bit, an' be all so good an' perfect just then; but they don't get wound up at all, so they don't go on bein' right, and so soon as they come out they're just as wrong as ever. Sunday, if 'tis what it ought to be, is a kind o' windin'-up day.

"I like to think that 'tis the *first* day o' the week; an' depend 'pon it, my friends, there's a deal depends 'pon the beginning o' things. Folks say sometimes, 'All's well that ends well;' and they patch up all kinds of ugly old sores with that plaster. I don't believe it one bit. If a thing don't begin well and go on well 'tisn't all well whatever kind of endin' it got. I s'pose the penitent thief ended well—he went to heaven; but that did'nt pay back what he had stolen, and it didn't mend all the harm he'd done. I'd rather have the 'well' at the other end too; I would. There'd be some truth if folks said, 'Well begun is half well done.' If you've got a good Sunday, you've got half a good week, I reckon. The old Sabbath o' the Jews was 'pon the last day o' the week, like as if they couldn't anyhow keep the law, an' so they finished up the week with all their sacrifices an' prayers. But now we Christians have got a Saviour Whose Name is called Jesus because He can *'save His people from their sins.'* An' so we come up 'pon the first day o' the week to get help an' strength to go through it all right—like as if we took hold o' that Blessed One Who is able to keep us from falling.

"Now good Sundays, like every thing else that is good, don't come o' their own accord. 'Tis only weeds an' crabs an' bramble-bushes that 'll grow if you let things alone. If you want flowers an' fruits you must dig an' plant an' work for 'em: and nobody is fool enough to expect 'em without. But in religion folks are fools enough a'most for anything, an' expect to pick up pearls o' great price without divin' for 'em, an' to get fat without eatin' anything. Good Sundays don't come anyhow, they are things that are made. An' every man has got to make his own. You can't order 'em ready-made o' the preacher.

"I reckon that's very much o' what the Lord Jesus meant when He said, *'Take heed how ye hear.'* Whatever it means, an' whatever it don't mean, it means this plain enough—*Don't hear anyhow.* You see that was the way with the ground that didn't prosper—it took the seed all anyhow. There was the way-side: it let the seed come just as it could, and o' course it all got trodden underfoot or was eaten up by the fowls, an' not a grain was left. An' then I daresay Brother Way-side went complainin' that he couldn't get any good under that preacher. There was the weedy-ground, too, let it fall in anyhow among the thorns an' thistles, an' they grew up an' choked it. An' I shouldn't wonder but Sister Weedy-ground whispered to Brother Way-side very piously, that for her part she did wish they had a preacher that would stir them up. Then there was Mister Stony-ground who liked it very much, an' nodded to everybody over the nice sermon, but when the sun was up, that is when dinner-time came, he could hardly remember the text. They all heard: but they were *anyhow* hearers. But there was dear old Father Good-ground, whenever he heard the Word it got in an' went down an' took root and sprang up an' bare fruit an' brought forth a hundred fold— such wonderful crops o' love an' joy an' peace that set all the folks a-scratchin' their heads however he could manage it! Yet it was no such great secret; *he got ready beforehand,*—that was all. He prepared for the seed. He'd have been weedy-ground, too, only he had been down on his knees an' pulled up the chokin' cares an' Saturday's worries; he had picked out the stones an' had ploughed up the field an' had given the seed a chance, that was all, an' so he got a harvest. You see there was the same Sower, an' the same seed, an' yet it was only the ground that was got ready beforehand that got any good.

"So, friends, if we don't take heed about it we shall be one o' these *anyhow hearers*. Ah! I'm 'fraid I shall hold up the lookin'-glass to a good many if I begin to tell what he's like. Well, he begins the Sunday an hour later than any other day, because 'tis the Lord's day. Other days are his own, an' he would be ashamed to take an hour out o' them; but the Lord's day he may do what he likes with, because it isn't his own. Then 'tis all a scramble to dress an' have breakfast an' be off to chapel. He comes along wonderin' if he's very late. If he were in time he might wonder, for everybody else would. Or perhaps he has got too hardened to mind that, so he comes along thinkin' o' nothing in particular. Then he gets into his place ready to listen, if the preacher can get his attention, but just so ready to dream away half-an-hour—that is, if he don't sleep it away,—or else lettin' his eyes go flittin' over the House o' God, pitchin' here an' there for a minute,

M

an' then off again, like a butterfly. I often meet him when I'm goin' home, an' he'll sigh as if he ought to be pitied more than scolded about it, an' complain that he was so troubled with wanderin' thoughts. Why o' course he was—what else could he expect? That, or something else, would be sure to spoil all the good, for he had not taken any heed about it. His mind was all full o' thorns an' thistles,—how could he expect to gather grapes an' figs?

"I really can't abide to hear folks talk about it as they do. 'Ah,' they say, 'it's natural, you know, for me to be so anxious.' Or else it is—'I really am so wearied, and you must make allowances for dispositions an' folks' nature. Pooh! nature an' natural! Why, if it hadn't been natural to hear anyhow, the Lord would never have told us to *take heed*. A gentleman comes up to his gardener expectin' a pretty show o' flowers an' fruits, but he finds the place all covered over with weeds an' things. An' so soon as ever he begins to talk to the gardener about it, the man sets off sighin',—'Please, Sir, 'tis quite natural for it to be so, and you must make allowances for nature.' Then the master can't stand it any longer,—t'was bad enough before, but this is too bad. 'Natural;' he says, 'o' course 'tis natural. And just because it would'nt go right of it's own self, I put you to look after it.' Friends, things won't come right without being made to; an' we must make 'em to, or else we shall find ourselves out in the darkness, with the rest o' the wicked and unprofitable servants. O' course, there 'd be things the gardener couldn't help; blight an' frosts an' drought; an' old an' tired folks 'll go to sleep, specially if the preachers help 'em to. If folks sleep when I'm a preachin', I say to myself 'Come, Dan'el, wake up;' for if the man in the pulpit is asleep, they in the pews 'll soon follow.

"But for all that, there are things we can do, an' we must. I do believe the first thing is this here, *Come in time.* Do you remember what is wrote down in the Gospel o' Luke, in the eighth chapter an' the fortieth verse? There's a secret for hearin' well. '*The people gladly received Him: for they were all waiting for Him.*' That's it: 'they were all waitin' for Him.' They didn't come rushin' in after He had come, makin' everybody lose a word or two while they turned round to see who it was, an' distractin' the mind o' that Blessed Preacher. That's the first 'take heed,' if you want to hear well: take heed an' come in time. If you come in after they're begun to sing, you'll be like John Trundle when he's late with his fiddle; he's too late to screw it an' scrape it into tune with the rest, so 'tis all flat an' dismal all through the service, and puts everybody else out o' tune too. O' course you would'nt come in durin' prayer: that's a real sin, I do count—when all the rest is tryin' to lift their thoughts up to Heaven, for somebody to come in a-draggin' 'em all down to earth again, an' making 'em forget the King o' Glory for to open their eyes an' see who 'tis come patterin' into the place! If the devil was to come to chapel, (an' I b'lieve he do come now an' then,) I'm sure he'd come in while they were prayin' an' he'd push past everybody up to his own corner, an' if he could knock over a hat or a pair o' pattens 'twould please 'em all the more.

"I don't believe in forms an' ceremonies; not a bit. A little bit o' heart is a fine passle better than a place full o' dead forms, though you sing 'em lovely. But I'm sure our Father in Heaven cares for the looks o' things. He wouldn't make a tree good for food without makin' it 'pleasant to the eyes.' The Book says, '*Strength and Beauty are in His sanctuary.* And now seemin' to me like as if this comin' late and lookin' all about, an' hearin' anyhow is a sort o' chippin' off the beauty an' spoilin' it all. An' then we spoil the beauty for ourselves more than for anybody else. Why some of us, my friends, would think that it was a new preacher come if instead o' hurryin' and scurryin' up to chapel, we'd only start from home a quarter of an hour sooner, an' come along the road a-thinkin' about the Lord.

"Then when he is come into the place, let a man have a bit o' prayer for his own self, and askin' the Lord to bless the preacher. It 'll do more good than whisperin' to your neighbour or starin' all about the place. When I got a cold in my head, singin' do seem to be all out o' tune, an' flowers haven't got a bit o' smell, an' I can't taste anything. I fancy the fault is in the things theirselves till the cold is gone; then I can see that it was all in my own-self. Let us only *take* heed about it, an' 'tis wonderful how different it 'll be! There's a fair half o' right hearin' in that they '*gladly received Him; for they were all waitin' for Him.*'

"Another 'take heed' that will help us is this: Let a man *take heed that* he hears *for his own soul an' for his own* good. 'Tis'nt much to listen just to see how the preacher will manage his text. We've come to get a blessing from the Lord. I was reading over the eighth o' Luke a day or two ago, and I couldn't help thinkin' about it—how everybody wanted Jesus for His own self! And how they all wanted Him different, each for his own case. There was the little boat tossing about 'pon the lake in the dark; the winds howlin' round 'em, an' the waves goin' hissin' past 'em, when Jesus comes, and in a minute He quiets winds an' waves an' their fears too. But then that was nothing to the man who had a legion o' devils in him. They were there when the wind blew a gale, an' when it was a dead calm. So Jesus comes to speak to him, an' make him whole. Then over the other side, Jairus' little maid lay a-dyin', an' they can't think o' storms, or anything else but their own trouble; and he besought Jesus to come and heal his little daughter. And then there was the poor woman who was full of her own need, and kept whisperin' to herself, '*If I may but touch His garment, I shall be whole*'—and she put forth her old trembling hand to take Him as she wanted.

"Now that is 'zactly as it ought to be when we go up on a Sunday; everybody must take heed an' find in Jesus what they want. Bless His dear Name, there's love for everybody in Him now, just so much as there was then! And there's help for every want, just so much as ever. That's it, let a man come up sayin', 'Now to-day I must get the Lord to strengthen my withered arm, or loose my tongue, or to make me clean.' Let them that have been worried come up a thinkin', 'Now to-day, whoever else is blest an' whatever else anybody may get, I want to cast all my care 'pon the Lord, and to get a fresh stock o' patience an' quiet trust.' Why a man can't help havin' a good Sunday when he hears about Jesus, and he begins to take hold o' his Blessed Lord all for his own-self. Let us come up seekin' Jesus just as we need Him. I believe one reason why the sick people had so much faith to be healed, was because they knew exactly what they wanted, an' because they wanted it with all their heart. And if folks would set themselves askin' for a bit: 'Now this mornin' what do I want Jesus to do for me?' an' if they wanted it with all their hearts, we shouldn't have a dull Sunday very often. They'd find Jesus with the loaves an' fishes even when it was a desert place, and when the poor preacher could give them nothing to eat.

"There is another 'take heed' that we must all look after: *Take heed an' beware o' the fowls*. There's all sorts an' sizes. There's times when one kind do mischief, an' there's times when another kind come plaguin' us. You know there's some that follow the sower while he is sowin', close to his heels,—pigeons an' sparrows; an' a little further back the rooks are busy, eatin' up the seed a'most before 'tis sown. Ah, we must beware o' these! Like when Abraham was bringin' his sacrifice before God, they come down upon our service, an' we must drive them away.

"Small birds do every bit so much mischief as any. Busy little things! they spoil many a good sermon. There are lots o' folks, if they can only light upon a word or a thought of the preacher's that they don't quite agree with or that isn't quite right, all the good is eaten up in a moment. All they think of is nothing but that, an' they'll go talkin' about it more than all the good things put together. Now this is worse than the fowls, for they never do like that. They'll scrape over a bushel o' dirt to find a grain o' corn, but these people 'll fling away a bushel o' good seed if they can but find a bit o' grit; and they'll hold it up an' show to everybody an' crow over it like a young bantam that's just a-feelin' his spurs. Other folks can't get any good if the preacher's manner isn't up to the latest fashion. But 'tis a sure sign o' weakness and bad health when folks are so dainty about their meat that their appetite's upset by the pattern o' the plates an' dishes.

"Then there's other fowls that come when the sower is gone. Fowls by the wayside; fowls out in the streets and on the way home. The Egyptian baker dreamt that the fowls eat the baked meats off his head as he went along. Now, if he had gone loitering along, hangin' about for a word with everybody, folks might have called him a nice friendly fellow, but I don't wonder that his master hanged him for a bad baker. And we shan't carry much o' the baked meats home with us unless we take heed o' the fowls. If the devil happened to be busy, we should tempt him to steal by our talkin' about everybody and everything all the way home. Put up your scare-crow to drive off these fowls. Anything will do for that; only let us try to keep them off, and they'll fly.

"Then there are the *weeds*: the chokin' weeds. Sunday, 'tis all going to be so nice an' beautiful, like my little bit of a garden when I've just done it up. Monday, 'tis all thick with weeds an' choked with wild stuff, like a place that hadn't been touched for a year. 'Tis like when I've been ridin' along in the train, an' I could look out o' the window, an' see the trees and the fields and now and then a glimpse o' the sea, and you're just a-thinkin' how pretty it all is when up comes a bank right in front and shuts all out, an' there's nothing there but the cuttin' o' rock an' earth, if 'tisn't a dark tunnel. Well, I find the best way is to come home tryin' to find something *to do* in the sermon; something to be prayed for, or prayed against, or to be thought about: for after all, friends, God's truth is worth to us only what we do with it. Seed is hard an' dead till you sow it. And the **Truth is dead words** till it is done. A man may tell me all about the road to Penzance an' all about the things that happened there, an' about the great folks who live alongside of it. But that won't take me there. I must get up and walk.

"Now, friends, if we can do this here, seemin'

to me, it'll be all well then. For we shall come up ready to hear—we shall go on to hear for our own selves; and we shall come home again to try and do what we have heard. Now let a man have a Sunday like that, and he'll be a long way on for having a good week. I can mind, when I was up to London, I was goin' along the noisy streets with crowds o' people about me, an' the roar an' rattle o' carts an' things, when all of a sudden there in the din and bustle I came to a lovely little garden. The flowers were growin' there beautiful, and a fountain was playin' makin' rainbows in the sunshine, and the trees were fresh and green, and the birds chirped to each other, an' flew about the place. 'Ah,' I said to myself, 'they can keep all this right here in the heart o' the busy city!' And that's just how we can carry Sunday with us, friends, all through the week. Cares an' worries and busy work will come about us, and keep a comin'; but for all that, in the heart we can keep a little garden o' the Lord, where the good seed bears sweet fruit, and the trees o' the Lord's own plantin' grow—planted by the rivers o' waters; an' where the singin' o' birds is heard, an' where very often the voice o' the Lord God Himself is heard, walkin' even in the heat o' our busy day."

WORKS BY THE SAME AUTHOR.

MISTER HORN AND HIS FRIENDS; or, GIVERS AND GIVING. 18mo. Price One Shilling.

"It has seldom fallen to our lot to read a little book so fresh, so vigorous, so racy. We do not know whether to admire most its combined humour and pathos, the perfect naturalness of the narrative, or its sound and wholesome moral. For pungent, pithy plainness of speech, it is quite equal to Mr. Spurgeon's most popular work, 'John Ploughman's Talk.' the book is written to enforce and illustrate the maxim *a man ought to think as much about giving as about getting.* It would be difficult to name a volume so likely to make men of this opinion as 'Mister Horn and his Friends.'"—*Christian Miscellany.*

"This is a spicy book on giving, and is written with admirable point, humour, and pungency. It is the very best thing of its class we have ever seen, including two or three of no ordinary power by our American cousins. If you knew a stingy professor, who wants enlargement of mind and of heart, send him a copy of this book. If it does not prove an effective cure, you may give him up as absolutely hopeless. This book deserves a wide circulation."—*Irish Evangelist.*

JOHN TREGENOWETH; HIS MARK. A Cornish Story. Royal 16mo. With Illustrations. Price One Shilling.

"The story of John Tregenoweth is a very touching one, and is told with great pathos and power. . . . The history of the hero powerfully enforces the great lesson of temperance. . . . It is a capital book for our young folk."—*Methodist Temperance Magazine.*

"This is a most touching story, admirably told, and worthy to rank with 'Jessica's First Prayer,' 'Little Meg,' and other books which will always be favourites as long as the fount of human feeling remains undried in human hearts. Then the story powerfully enforces that great lesson of temperance which was never so much needed in England as now. This story would be a capital 'Reading' for a Band of Hope, or Sunday-School Entertainment, and it should be given away in large numbers by those who are anxious to promote the spread of true temperance and healthy literature amongst the people."—*Children's Advocate.*

CAN I BE SAVED? Demy 16mo., 32pp., with Illustrations. Fortieth Thousand. Price One Penny.

"Here is the very thing for wayside distribution on road and rail and river. We are pleased to hear that ten thousand of them were distributed at the Royal Agricultural Show at Bedford."—*The Methodist.*

THE STORY OF BILLY BRAY. 16 pp. Price 4s. per 100.

A GOOD OLD PRESCRIPTION: A CURE FOR CARE. 8 pp. Price 2s. per 100.

WHAT THE LARK SANG TO ROBERT MORLEY. 8 pp. Price 2s. per 100.

GETTING SAVED: A TRACT FOR THOSE WHO ARE SEEKING CHRIST. 8 pp. Price 2s. per 100.

MY OLD FRIEND JOHN. 8 pp. Price 2s. per 100.

LONDON: WESLEYAN CONFERENCE OFFICE,
2, CASTLE STREET, CITY ROAD,
AND 66, PATERNOSTER ROW.

OPINIONS OF THE PRESS,

ABOUT

„Daniel Quorm, and his Religious Notions."

"There is a reality and freshness about the book that will be sure to render it a favourite wherever it is known. . . . We heartily thank the author for this fresh and readable book."—*Christian Age.*

"Rich in Cornish anecdotes and passages from the simple annals of the poor, Mr. Pearse's book must be popular, and being full of Gospel truth cannot fail to be useful."—*Sword and Trowel.*

"This is what our American friends would call a 'live' book. It has, too, not only plenty of 'go' in it, but its exuberant vitality is of a most infectious kind. The reader could hardly fall asleep over it if he would! The racy illustrations of Mr. Tresidder are every way worthy of the text, and that is saying a good deal."—*The Baptist.*

"Mr. Pearse can describe character and scenery with equal precision and power; and in the present volume his efforts are well supported by numerous illustrations. The portraits of Daniel himself, and of his humble friends, are very life-like, both in the pages of the author, and in the pictures of the artist."—*Daily Free Press.*

"Daniel Quorm is a Cornish Methodist Class-leader and a village shoemaker. . . . It is not a preposterous exaggeration to say that Daniel Quorm, as Mr. Pearse has made him, has a way of setting forth the religion of faith which might well be envied by professional men. . . . Daniel Quorm can be as smart in the Class-room as in the market; because the topics of the Class-room are to him as full of life and immediate interest as the topics of the market. . . . Mr. Pearse's charming book is illustrated by a brother Cornishman, Mr. Charles Tresidder, with admirable skill."—*The Empire.*

"'Daniel Quorm' is a worthy companion to 'Mister Horn.' Indeed, we should say it is the best production of the author's pen. . . . Those who invest two shillings and sixpence in the purchase of this book will not regret the transaction."—*Methodist New-Connexion Magazine.*

"'Daniel Quorm' is a most wonderful character. . . . His 'religious notions' are so just, and of such intrinsic value, and withal expressed in so quaint, and shrewd and practical a manner, that we should like for all our readers, at least for a time, to become members of 'Brother Dan'el's' class. This book has our heartiest recommendation."—*Bible-Christian Magazine.*

"Mr. Pearse writes with a sure pen, with a keen appreciation of humour, and a wide knowledge of human nature. . . . Handsomely got up, well illustrated. His characters, when elaborated, are not mere shadows, but stand boldly out as people who live, move, and talk. . . . Bright sketches well calculated to serve Methodism, wherever known. . . . The volume deserves the widest circulation."—*Watchman.*

"This book is worthy of the special notice of the Class-leaders of Methodism, whilst all devout Christians may find in it, amidst beauty, humour, and pathos, words profitable for direction and instruction."—*Methodist Recorder.*

"We warmly commend it as one of the most bright, sparkling, racy books that we have seen for many a day. Mr. Pearse has rare power in sketching character. Some of the touches in this book could hardly be exceeded.—*Irish Evangelist.*

"The readers of this Magazine have no need to be told how well worth knowing is 'Daniel Quorm,' and how full of shrewdness, pith and point are his 'religious notions.'. . . We will only add that the getting-up of this book is most tasteful and attractive. . . . The illustrations are vigorous and life-like."—*City-Road Magazine.*

PUBLICATIONS
OF THE
WESLEYAN CONFERENCE OFFICE.

NEW BOOKS AND NEW EDITIONS.

The Doctrine of **a Future Life as contained in the Old** Testament Scriptures. Being the Fifth Lecture on the Foundation of John Fernley, Esq. Delivered in Wesley Chapel, Camborne, July 28th, 1873. By John Dury Geden, Tutor in Hebrew and Classics, Didsbury College, Manchester. Demy 8vo. Price 1s.

The Life of James Dixon, **D.D., Wesleyan Minister.** Written by his Son, Richard Watson Dixon, M.A., Minor Canon in Carlisle Cathedral. With three Portraits, and a Vignette of his College. Crown 8vo. Price 6s.

Memorials of the Life and Labours of the Rev. **William** Shaw, for twenty-six years head of the Wesleyan Missions in South East Africa. By his Son. Crown 8vo. With a Portrait, a Map, etc. Price 7s. 6d.

Missionary Anecdotes, Sketches, Facts, and **Incidents.** Relative to the Christian Heathen and the Labours of the Gospel in various parts of the World. By the Rev. William Moister. Crown 8vo. Price 5s.

The History of Methodism **in Macclesfield, Cheshire.** By the Rev. Benjamin Smith. Crown 8vo. Price 5s.

Recollections of My Own Life **and Times. By Thomas** Jackson. Edited by the Rev. B. Frankland, B.A. With an Introduction by Thomas O. Summers, D.D. 8vo. Portrait. Crown 8vo. Cloth. Price 7s. 6d.

Class-Meetings in Relation to the Design and Success of Methodism. By the Rev. William Unsworth. Foolscap 8vo. Price 1s.

Society Meetings in Wesleyan Methodism. By the Rev. Joseph Earnshaw. Foolscap 8vo. Price 1s.

Scenes from the Life of Nehemiah; or, Chapters for Christian Workers. Foolscap 8vo. Price 1s.

Daniel Quorm and his Religious Notions. By the Rev. Mark Guy Pearse. Crown 8vo. Numerous Illustrations. Cloth extra. Second Edition. Price 2s. 6d.

Christian Work for Gentle Hands: Thoughts on Female Agency in the Church of God. By the Rev. JOHN DWYER. Third Edition. Price 1s. 6d.

Memorials of the Rev. William Toase: Consisting principally of Extracts from his Journals and Correspondence, Illustrative of the Rise and Progress of Methodism in France and the Channel Islands. Compiled by a FRIEND. With an INTRODUCTION by the Rev. WILLIAM ARTHUR, M.A. Crown 8vo. Price 3s. 6d.

How to Pray and What to Pray For. An Exposition of the Lord's Prayer and Christ's Introductory Sayings. By the Rev. EDWARD JEWITT ROBINSON. Crown 8vo. Price 5s.

For Ever! An Essay on Eternal Punishment. By the Rev. MARSHALL RANDLES. Second Edition, Revised and Enlarged. Crown 8vo. Price 4s.

Ecclesiastical Principles and Polity of the Wesleyan Methodists. The whole compiled by WILLIAM PEIRCE, and revised by FREDERICK J. JOBSON, D.D. Third Edition. Royal 8vo., cloth, 15s.; half morocco, cloth sides, 20s.

> This work contains a correct Transcript of all the published Laws and Regulations of the Wesleyan Methodist Connexion, from its first organization to the present time, and affords full and authentic information on the History, Discipline, and Economy of Methodism.

COMMENTARIES, DICTIONARIES, &c.,

ILLUSTRATIVE OF THE HOLY SCRIPTURES.

Aids to Daily Meditation: being Practical Reflections and Observations on a Passage of Scripture for each Day in the Year. Crown 8vo., cloth, red edges. Price 3s. 6d.

The Holy Bible: with Notes, Critical, Explanatory, and Practical. By the Rev. JOSEPH BENSON. With Maps and a Portrait of the Author. Six Volumes, Imperial 8vo., cloth, red edges. Price £3 3s. Sold also in Separate Volumes, cloth, red edges. Price 10s. 6d. each.

A Biblical and Theological Dictionary: Illustrative of the Old and New Testament. By the Rev. JOHN FARRAR. With a Map of Palestine and numerous Engravings. Crown 8vo. Price 3s. 6d.

An Ecclesiastical Dictionary: *Explanatory of the History, Antiquities, Heresies, Sects, and Religious Denominations of the Christian Church.* By the Rev. JOHN FARRAR. Crown 8vo. Price 5s.

The Proper Names of the Bible; *their Orthography, Pronunciation, and Signification.* With a brief Account of the Principal Persons, and a Description of the principal Places. By the Rev. JOHN FARRAR. 18mo. Price 1s. 6d.

A Commentary on the Old and New Testament; containing copious notes, Theological, Historical, and Critical; with Improvements and Reflections. By the Rev. JOSEPH SUTCLIFFE, M.A. Imperial 8vo., cloth, marbled edges. Price 12s. 6d.

A Biblical and Theological Dictionary, *Explanatory of the History, Manners, and Customs of the Jews, and Neighbouring Nations.* With an Account of the most remarkable Places mentioned in Sacred Scripture; An Exposition of the principal Doctrines of Christianity; and Notices of Jewish and Christian Sects and Heresies. By the Rev. RICHARD WATSON. Royal 8vo., cloth, red edges. Price 12s. 6d.

An Exposition of the Gospels of St. Matthew and St. Mark, and of some other detached parts of Scripture. By the Rev. RICHARD WATSON. Demy 8vo. Price 6s. 12mo. Price 3s. 6d.

The New Testament, with Explanatory Notes. By the Rev. JOHN WESLEY. With the Author's last Corrections.
 Pocket Edition. 18mo. Price 2s.
 Large-Type Edition. 8vo. Price 4s.
 Library Edition, fine paper. Demy 8vo. Price 6s.

An Exposition of St. Paul's Epistle to the Romans. By the Rev. HENRY W. WILLIAMS. Crown 8vo. Price 6s.

An Exposition of the Epistle to the Hebrews. By the Rev. HENRY W. WILLIAMS. Crown 8vo. Price 6s.

The Incarnate Son of God: *or, the History of the Life and Ministry of the Redeemer;* arranged, generally, according to Greswell's Harmony of the Gospels. By the Rev. HENRY W. WILLIAMS. Crown 8vo. Price 4s.

Scripture compared with Scripture. A Plan for Daily Bible Reading throughout the Year. Arranged by E. G. C. Price 1s., limp cloth, gilt edges, s.d.

THEOLOGY.

Bunting (J.) Sermons by the Rev. Jabez Bunting, D.D.
Two Volumes. Crown 8vo., cloth, red edges. Price 10s. 6d.
Volume Two is sold separately. Price 3s. 6d.

Dunn (L. R.) The Mission of the Spirit; or the Office
and Work of the Comforter in human Redemption. By the Rev. LEWIS R. DUNN, Minister of the Methodist Episcopal Church, U.S. Edited by the Rev. JOSEPH BUSH. Crown 8vo. Price 2s.

Edmondson (J.) Sermons on Important Subjects; with
an Introduction by the Rev. T. JACKSON. Two Volumes. Crown 8vo. Price 6s.

Fletcher (J.) An Appeal to Matter of Fact and Com-
mon Sense; or, a Rational Demonstration of Man's Corrupt and Lost Estate. By the Rev. JOHN FLETCHER. 12mo. Price 2s.

Fletcher (J.) Five Checks to Antinomianism. By the Rev. JOHN FLETCHER. 12mo. Price 4s. 6d.

Fletcher (J.) The Works of the Rev. John Fletcher;
with his Life, by the Rev. JOSEPH BENSON. Complete in Nine Volumes. 12mo. Price £1 11s. 6d.

The Holy Catholic Church, the Communion of Saints:
Being the FERNLEY LECTURE for 1873. With Notes, and Essays on The History of Christian Fellowship, and on The Origin of "High Church" and "Broad Church" Theories. By the Rev. BENJAMIN GREGORY. Demy 8vo., 290 pages, Paper Covers. Price 3s. 6d.; Cloth gilt lettered, 4s. 6d.

Hannah (J.) Introductory Lectures on the Study of
Christian Theology; with Outlines of Lectures on the Doctrines of Christianity. By the late Rev. JOHN HANNAH, D.D.; to which is prefixed a Memoir of Dr. Hannah, by the Rev. W. B. POPE. Crown 8vo. Price 6s.

Jackson (T.) The Duties of Christianity; theoretically
and practically considered. By the Rev. THOMAS JACKSON. Second Edition. Crown 8vo. Price 4s.

Jackson (T.) The Institutions of Christianity, exhibited
in their Scriptural Character and Practical Bearing. By the Rev. THOMAS JACKSON. Crown 8vo. Price 5s.

Jackson (T.) **The Providence of God, viewed in the Light**
of Holy Scripture. By the Rev. THOMAS JACKSON. New Edition, with Improvements. Crown 8vo. Price 4s.

Jackson (T.) **The Christian armed against Infidelity.**
A Collection of Treatises in Defence of Divine Revelation. Foolscap 8vo. Price 2s.

McAfee (D.) **The Pillar and Ground of the Truth.**
Twelve Sermons on the Fundamental Truths of Christianity. By the Rev. DANIEL MCAFEE. With a Preface, by the Rev. WILLIAM ARTHUR, M.A. Crown 8vo. With Portrait. Price 6s.

Pope (W. B.) **The Kingdom and Reign of Christ.**
Twenty-one Discourses delivered in the Chapel of the Wesleyan Theological Institution, Didsbury. By the Rev. WILLIAM B. POPE, Theological Tutor. Foolscap 8vo. Price 5s.

Pope (W. B.) **The Person of Christ: Dogmatic, Scrip-**
tural, Historical. The Fernley Lecture of 1871. With two additional Essays on the Biblical and Ecclesiastical Development of the Doctrine, and Illustrative Notes. By the Rev. W. B. POPE, Theological Tutor, Didsbury College. 8vo. Price 7s.

Prest (C.) **The Witness of the Holy Spirit.** By the Rev.
CHARLES PREST. Third Edition. Crown 8vo., cloth, red edges. Price 3s.

Thomas (J. W.) **The Lord's Day; or, the Christian**
Sabbath: its History, Obligation, Importance, and Blessedness. By the Rev. JOHN WESLEY THOMAS. Crown 8vo. Price 3s. 6d.

Treffry (R.) **Inquiry into the Doctrine of the Eternal**
Sonship of our Lord Jesus Christ. By the Rev. RICHARD TREFFRY, Jun. Crown 8vo. Price 6s.

Treffry (R.) **The Atonement viewed in Relation to**
Scripture and Reason. In a series of Letters to a Friend. By the Rev. RICHARD TREFFRY, Jun. 18mo. Price 2s.

Watson (R.) **Sermons and Sketches of Sermons.** By
the Rev. RICHARD WATSON.
Three Volumes, demy 8vo. Price 18s.
Three Volumes, post 8vo. Price 10s. 6d.

Watson (R.) **Theological Institutes; or, a View of the**
Evidences, Doctrines, Morals, and Institutions of Christianity. By the Rev. RICHARD WATSON.
Three Volumes, demy 8vo. Price 18s.
Four Volumes, royal 18mo. Price 11s.

Watson (R.) *The Works of the Rev. Richard Watson.*
With his Memoirs by the Rev. THOMAS JACKSON.
>Thirteen Volumes, demy 8vo. Price £3 18s.
>Thirteen Volumes, post 8vo. Price £2 5s. 6d.

Wesley (J.) *Sermons on Several Occasions.* By the Rev. JOHN WESLEY, M.A. With a Life of the Author by the Rev. JOHN BEECHAM, D.D.
>Three Vols., crown 8vo. Price 7s. 6d.
>Fine Edition, three Vols., post 8vo. Price 10s. 6d.
>Library Edition, three Vols., demy 8vo. Price 18s.

Wesley (J.) *The Prose Works of the Rev. John Wesley,* M.A. Edited by the Rev. THOMAS JACKSON. This Edition contains all the Latest Corrections of the Author; and includes the Life of Mr. Wesley by the Rev. JOHN BEECHAM, D.D.
>Library Edition, Fourteen Volumes, demy 8vo. Price £4 4s.
>Cheap Edition, Fourteen Volumes, post 8vo. Price £2 2s.

Wiseman (L. H.) *Christ in the Wilderness; or, Practical* Views of our Lord's Temptation. By the Rev. LUKE H. WISEMAN, M.A. Crown 8vo. Price 3s. 6d.

BIOGRAPHY.

Agar (B.) *Memoirs of Mrs. Benjamin Agar, of York;* With Extracts from her Diary and Correspondence. By the Rev. LUKE H. WISEMAN, M.A., Author of "Christ in the Wilderness," "Men of Faith," &c. Crown 8vo. Price 2s. 6d.

Asbury (F.) *Bishop Asbury:* A Biographical Study for Christian Workers. By the Rev. F. W. BRIGGS. Crown 8vo. With Portrait. Price 3s. 6d.

Alpine Missionary (The); *or, the Life of J. L. Rostan,* Missionary Pastor in France, Switzerland, and the Channel Isles. By the Rev. MATTHEW LELIEVRE. Translated from the French Edition, by the Rev. A. J. FRENCH, B.A. With a Portrait. Crown 8vo. Price 3s. 6d.

Bamford (J.) *The Disciple among the Poor:* Memorials of Mr. John Bamford, of Shardlow. By his Son, the Rev. JOHN M. BAMFORD. Crown 8vo. Price 3s. With Photographic Portrait, 3s. 6d.

Bohler (P.) **Memorials of the Life of Peter Bohler,**
Bishop of the Church of the United Brethren. By the Rev. J. P.
LOCKWOOD. With an Introduction by the Rev. THOMAS JACKSON; and
with a finely engraved Portrait. Crown 8vo. Price 2s. 6d.

Bramwell (W.) **The Christian Minister in Earnest.** A
Memoir of the Rev. William Bramwell; containing Extracts from his
Correspondence, and a Delineation of his Personal and Ministerial
Character. By the Rev. THOMAS HARRIS. Royal 18mo., gilt edges.
Price 3s. Cheap Edition. Royal 32mo. Price 1s.

Bumby (J. H.) **The Life of the Rev. John H. Bumby.**
With a brief History of the Progress of the Wesleyan Mission in New
Zealand. By the Rev. ALFRED BARRETT. With a Portrait. 12mo.
Price 3s.

Bunting (William M.) **Memorials of.** Being Selections
from his Sermons, Letters, and Poems. Edited by the Rev. G. STRINGER
ROWE. With a Biographical Introduction by THOMAS PERCIVAL
BUNTING. Crown 8vo. Price 3s. 6d.

Carvosso (W.) **Memoirs of William Carvosso.** Written
by himself, and edited by his Son. With a Portrait. Royal 18mo.
Price 2s. 6d. Cheap Edition. Royal 32mo. Price 1s.

Clarke (A.) **The Life of Dr. Adam Clarke.** By the
Rev. Dr. ETHERIDGE. With a Portrait. Post 8vo. Price 3s. 6d.
Cheap Edition. Royal 32mo. Price 1s. 6d.

Coke (T.) **The Life of Thomas Coke.** By the Rev. Dr.
ETHERIDGE. With a Portrait. Post 8vo. Price 3s. 6d.
Cheap Edition. Royal 32mo. Price 1s. 6d.

Cryer (Mrs.) **Holy Living;** Exemplified in the Life of
Mrs. Mary Cryer, Wife of the Rev. Thomas Cryer, Wesleyan Mission-
ary to India. By the Rev. ALFRED BARRETT. With Vignette Title and
Frontispiece. Foolscap 8vo. Price 3s.

Dixon (J.) **The Life of James Dixon, D.D., Wesleyan**
Minister. Written by his Son. RICHARD WATSON DIXON, M.A., Minor
Canon of Carlisle Cathedral; &c. With three Portraits of Dr. DIXON,
and a Vignette of his Birthplace. Crown 8vo. Price 7s. 6d.

Dixon (T.) **The Earnest Methodist.** A Memoir of the
late Mr. Thomas Dixon, of Grantham. By his Nephew, the Rev.
JOSEPH DIXON. Foolscap 8vo. With Portrait. Price 2s.

Entwisle (J.) **Memoir of the Rev. Joseph Entwisle:** with copious Extracts from his Journals and Correspondence, and Occasional Notices of Contemporary Events in the History of Methodism. By his Son. With a Portrait. Crown 8vo. Price 3s.

Fletcher (J.) **The Life of the Rev. John Fletcher.** By the Rev. JOSEPH BENSON. With a Portrait. 12mo. Price 3s. 6d. Cheap Edition. Royal 32mo. Price 1s.

Fletcher (Mrs.) **The Life of Mrs. Fletcher.** By the Rev. HENRY MOORE. With a Portrait. Crown 8vo. Price 3s. 6d. Cheap Edition. Royal 32mo. Price 1s.

George (E.) **Memoirs of Elizabeth George.** By the Rev. HENRY J. PIGGOTT, B.A. With a Portrait. Crown 8vo. Price 2s. 6d.

Grimshaw (W.), **Incumbent of Haworth.** By the Rev. R. SPENCE HARDY. Crown 8vo. Price 3s.

Hare (R. H.) **The Ministry and Character of Robert** Henry Hare, Wesleyan Minister. By JOHN MIDDLETON HARE, his Brother. Crown 8vo. With Portrait. Price 6s.

Hunt (J.) **The Life of John Hunt, Missionary to the** Cannibals in Fiji. By the Rev. GEORGE STRINGER ROWE. Limp cloth. Price 1s. 6d. With Portrait, cloth extra, 2s. 6d.

Jackson (T.) **Lives of Early Methodist Preachers.** Chiefly written by themselves. Edited with an Introductory Essay by the Rev. THOMAS JACKSON.
  Library Edition, Six Vols. Crown 8vo. Price 15s.
  Cheap Edition, Six Vols. Foolscap 8vo. Price 9s.

Jackson (T.) **Recollections of My Own Life and Times.** By THOMAS JACKSON. Edited by the Rev. B. FRANKLAND, B.A. With an Introduction and Postscript by G. OSBORN, D.D. With a Portrait. Crown 8vo. Price 5s.

M'Owan (P.) **A Man of God; or, Providence and Grace** Exemplified in a Memoir of the Rev. Peter M'Owan. Compiled chiefly from his Letters and Papers. By the Rev. JOHN M'OWAN. Edited by G. OSBORN, D.D. Crown 8vo. Price 5s.

Maxwell (Lady). **The Life of Darcy Lady Maxwell.** By the Rev. WILLIAM ATHERTON. With Selections from her Diary and Correspondence. Crown 8vo. Price 3s. 6d.

Miller (W. E.) *Life of the Rev. W. E. Miller.* By the Rev. Dr. DIXON. Foolscap 8vo. Price 2s.; limp cloth, 1s. 6d.

Nelson (J.) *The Journal of Mr. John Nelson.* Royal 18mo. Price 1s. 6d. Cheap Edition. Royal 32mo. Price 10d.

Newton (R.) *The Life of the Rev. Robert Newton, D.D.* By the Rev. THOMAS JACKSON. With a Portrait. Crown 8vo. Price 2s. 6d. Cheap Edition. Royal 32mo. Price 1s. 6d.

Newton (Mrs.) *Memorials of the Life of Mrs. Newton,* Wife of the late Rev. Robert Newton, D.D. By her DAUGHTER. Royal 18mo. Cloth, gilt edges. Price 2s. 6d.

Rogers (Mrs.) *The Experience and Spiritual Letters of* Mrs. Hester Ann Rogers. 18mo. Price 1s. 6d. Cheap Edition. Royal 32mo. Price 10d.

Rogers (Mrs.) *The Experience, Letters, and Journal of* Mrs. Hester Ann Rogers. In one Vol. 18mo., roan, embossed, gilt edges. Price 3s. 6d.

Smith (J.) *Memoirs of the Life, Character, and Labours* of the Rev. John Smith. By the Rev. R. TREFFRY, Jun. With an Introductory Essay by the Rev. Dr. DIXON. Royal 18mo. Price 3s. Cheap Edition, without the Introductory Essay. Price 1s.

Stoner (D.) *Memoirs of the Rev. David Stoner.* By the Rev. Dr. HANNAH and Mr. WILLIAM DAWSON. With a Portrait. 18mo. Price 2s. 6d. Cheap Edition. Royal 32mo. Price 1s.

Tackaberry (F.) *The Life and Labours of the Rev.* Fossey Tackaberry; with Notices of Methodism in Ireland. By the Rev. R. HUSTON. Second Edition. Crown 8vo. Price 3s.

Taylor (Michael C.) *Memoir of the Rev. M. C. Taylor.* With Extracts from his Correspondence. By the Rev. B. OULTIER. Crown 8vo. Price 2s. 6d.

Threlfall (W.) *Memorials of the Rev. W. Threlfall.* By the Rev. SAMUEL BROADBENT. 18mo. With Portrait. Price 1s. 6d.

Toase (W.) *Memorials of the Rev. William Toase.* Compiled by a Friend. With an Introduction by the Rev. WILLIAM ARTHUR, M.A. Crown 8vo. Price 3s. 6d.

Treffry (R.) *Memoirs of the Rev. R. Treffry, Jun.* With Select Remains, consisting of Sketches of Sermons, Essays, and Poetry. By his Father, the Rev. RICHARD TREFFRY. With a Portrait. 12mo. Price 4s. 6d.

Turner (N.) *The Pioneer Missionary;* or, the Life of the Rev. Nathaniel Turner, Missionary in New Zealand, Tonga, and Australasia. By his Son, the Rev. J. G. TURNER. Crown 8vo. With Portrait. Price 5s.

Watson (R.) *Memoirs of the Life and Writings of the* Rev. Richard Watson. By the Rev. THOMAS JACKSON. With a Portrait. Royal 18mo. Price 3s. 6d. 8vo. Price 6s.

Wesley (C.) *The Life of the Rev. Charles Wesley.* Comprising a Review of his Poetry; Sketches of the Rise and Progress of Methodism; with Notices of Contemporary Events and Characters. By the Rev. THOMAS JACKSON. With a Portrait. Crown 8vo. Price 3s. 6d.

Wesley (C.) *The Journal of the Rev. Charles Wesley.* With Selections from his Correspondence and Poetry, and an Introduction by the Rev. THOMAS JACKSON. Two Vols. Royal 18mo. Price 7s.

Wesley (J.) *The Life of the Rev. John Wesley.* By the Rev. RICHARD WATSON. With a Portrait. Royal 18mo. Price 3s. 6d. Cheap Edition. Royal 32mo. Price 1s. 4d.

Wesley (J.) *The Journals of the Rev. John Wesley.* Four Vols. 12mo. Price 10s.

Wesley (J.) *His Life and his Work.* By the Rev. M. LELIEVRE. Translated by the Rev. A. J. FRENCH. With a Portrait. Crown 8vo. Price 3s.

West (F. A.) *Memorials of the Rev. Francis A. West.* Being a Selection from his Sermons and Lectures. With a Biographical Sketch by one of his Sons, and Personal Recollections by the Rev. B. GREGORY. Crown 8vo. Price 4s.

Wood (J.) *The Life of the Rev. Joseph Wood.* With Extracts from his Diary. By the Rev. H. W. WILLIAMS. With a Portrait. Crown 8vo. Price 3s.

NEW BOOKS AND NEW EDITIONS,
SUITABLE FOR SUNDAY-SCHOOL LIBRARIES AND REWARDS.

Banks (J. S.) Three Indian Heroes: The Missionary;
The Soldier; The Statesman. By the Rev. J. S. BANKS. Fcap. 8vo. with Portrait of HAVELOCK. Price 1s. 6d.

Bleby (H.) The Stolen Children; A Narrative compiled from Authentic Sources, by the Rev. HENRY BLEBY, Author of "Death Struggles of Slavery." Foolscap 8vo., cloth, gilt edges, with Illustrations. Price 2s. 6d.

Briggs (F. W.) Chequer Alley: A Story of Successful Christian Work. By the Rev. FREDERICK W. BRIGGS. With an Introduction by the Rev. W. ARTHUR, M.A. Ninth Edition. Foolscap 8vo. Price 1s. 6d.

Gleanings in Natural History for Young People. Gathered from "Early Days." Royal 16mo. Profusely Illustrated. Price 1s. 6d.

Lessons from Noble Lives, and other Stories. Selected from "Early Days." Royal 16mo. Numerous Illustrations. Price 1s.

Lightwood (E.) Ancient Egypt: Its Monuments, Worship, and People. By the Rev. EDWARD LIGHTWOOD. Royal 16mo., numerous Illustrations. Price 1s.

Margery's Christmas Box. By RUTH ELLIOTT. Royal 16mo. Illustrations. Price 1s.

Montfort (Lillie.) Incidents in my Sunday-School Life. By LILLIE MONTFORT, Author of "My Class for Jesus." Foolscap 8vo. Price 2s.

Old Truths in New Lights. A Series of Sunday-School Addresses. By W. H. S. Foolscap 8vo. Numerous Illustrations. Price 1s. 6d.

Pearse (M. G.) Daniel Quorm and his Religious Notions. By the Rev. MARK GUY PEARSE. Crown 8vo. Numerous Illustrations. Cloth, gilt edges. Price 2s. 6d.

Pearse (M. G.) John Tregenoweth: His Mark. By the Rev. MARK GUY PEARSE. Royal 16mo., cloth. Illustrated. Price 1s.

Tatham (E.) *The Dream of Pythagoras, and Other*
Poems. By EMMA TATHAM. Fifth Edition, with Additional Pieces, and a MEMOIR, by the Rev. B. GREGORY, Author of the "Thorough Business Man," etc. Crown 8vo., cloth. Price 3s. 6d. French Morocco, extra gilt, and gilt edges. Price 7s. 6d.

Thomas (J. W.) *The Tower, the Temple, and the*
Minster: Historical and Biographical Associations of the Tower of London, St. Paul's Cathedral, and Westminster Abbey. By the Rev. J. W. THOMAS. Foolscap 8vo. Illustrated. Price 2s.

Thomas (J. W.) *William the Silent, Prince of Orange.*
A Biographical Study. By the Rev. J. W. THOMAS. Foolscap 8vo. With Portrait. Price 1s.

Waddy (E.) *The Father of Methodism.* A Sketch of the Life and Labours of the REV. JOHN WESLEY, A.M. For Young People. By EDITH WADDY. Foolscap 8vo. Numerous Illustrations. Price 1s. 6d.

Waddy, (E.) *A Year with the Wild Flowers.* An Introduction to the Study of English Botany. By EDITH WADDY. Royal 16mo. Numerous Illustrations. Gilt edges. Price 3s. 6d.

Yeames (J.) *Vignettes from English History.* By the Rev. JAMES YEAMES. First Series. From the Norman Conqueror to Henry IV. Royal 16mo. Numerous Illustrations. Price 1s.

Adeline. *Pictures from Memory:* By ADELINE. Selected from "Early Days." 18mo. Illustrated. Price 9d.

Adeline. *Helen Leslie: or, Truth and Error.* By Adeline. 18mo. Price 1s.

Barrett (A.) *The Boatman's Daughter.* A Narrative for the Learned and Unlearned. 18mo. Price 1s. 4d.

Crump (S.) *Soon and Safe.* A Few Words to the Young Folk. By the Rev. SIMPSON CRUMP. 18mo., Illustrated Price 9d.

Doncaster (J.) *Friendly Hints, addressed to the Youth*
of Both Sexes, on Mind, Morals, and Religion. By the Rev. JOHN DONCASTER. 18mo. Price 1s. 6d.

Facts and Incidents *Illustrative of the Scripture Doc-*
trines as set forth in the First and Second Catechisms of the Wesleyan Methodists. Second Edition. Crown 8vo. Price 3s. 6d.

Freddie Cleminson: The Brief Story of a Blessed Life.
By the Rev. T. MCCULLAGH. 18mo. With Portrait, and View of Methodist College, Belfast. Price 9d.

Gems of English Poetry: From Chaucer to the Present Time. Selected by Mrs. MARZIALS. Foolscap 8vo., gilt edges. Price 3s. 6d.

Hartley (J.) Hid Treasures and the Search for Them: being Lectures to Bible Classes. By the Rev. JOHN HARTLEY. Royal 18mo. Price 2s.

Hay (D.) A Father's Religious Counsels Addressed to his Son at School. By the Rev. DAVID HAY. 18mo. 1s.

Hay (D.) Home: or, the Way to Make Home Happy. By the Rev. DAVID HAY. With an Introduction by the Rev. ALFRED BARRETT. 18mo., gilt edges. Price 1s. 6d.

Huston (R.) Letters on the Distinguishing Excellence of Remarkable Scripture Personages. By the Rev. ROBERT HUSTON. 18mo. Price 1s. 6d.

Huston (R.) Cautions and Counsels Addressed to the Young. Enforced by Illustrations chiefly drawn from Scripture Narratives. 18mo. Price 1s. 6d.

Hudson (W.) This Transitory Life: Addresses designed to help Thoughtful YOUNG PERSONS correctly to estimate THE PRESENT WORLD and its AFFAIRS. By the Rev. WILLIAM HUDSON. Foolscap 8vo. Price 1s. 6d.

Leonard (G.) Life on the Waves; or Memorials of Captain GEORGE LEONARD. By the Rev. A. LANGLEY, Author of "The Reformer and Revival of Religion," etc. With Illustrations. 18mo. Price 1s.

Maunder (G.) Eminent Christian Philanthropists. Brief Biographical Sketches, designed especially as studies for the Young. By the Rev. GEORGE MAUNDER. Foolscap 8vo. Price 2s.

This Volume gives as Brief Biographical Sketches of

John Howard,	Granville Sharp,	David Nasmith,
Isaac Hopper,	Thomas Clarkson,	Elizabeth Fry,
James Hinton,	W. Wilberforce,	Thomas F. Buxton,
Edward Reynolds,	J. Butterworth,	Sarah Martin.
Robert Raikes,	William Allen,	

Mather (G.) *Lectures on the Sublime and Beautiful in*
Nature and Morals. By the Rev. GEORGE MATHER. Second Edition. Crown 8vo. Price 2s. 6d.

Parker (Mrs.) *Annals of the Christian Church.* From
the First to the Nineteenth Centuries. By MRS. PARKER. With Ten Portraits engraved on Steel. Crown 8vo. Price 3s. 6d.

Smith (B.) *Climbing: A Manual for the Young who*
desire to rise in Both Worlds. Crown 8vo., cloth extra. Fourth Edition. Revised and Enlarged. Price 2s. 6d.

Smith (B.) *The Power of the Tongue; or, Chapters*
for Talkers. By the Rev. BENJAMIN SMITH. Crown 8vo. Price 3s. 6d.

Smith (B.) *Sunshine in the Kitchen; or, Chapters for*
Maid Servants. By the Rev. BENJAMIN SMITH, Author of "Vice-Royalty," "Climbing," etc. Crown 8vo. Numerous Illustrations. Price 3s. 6d.

Smith (B.) *Vice-Royalty: or, Counsels respecting*
Government of the Heart: addressed especially to Young Men. By the Rev. BENJAMIN SMITH. Crown 8vo. Price 3s.

Smith (T.) *Youths of the Old Testament.* By the Rev.
THORNLEY SMITH. 18mo. Price 2s. 6d.

Smith (T.) *The Holy Child Jesus; or, the Early Life of*
Christ: Viewed in connection with the History, Chronology, and Archæology of the Times. Foolscap 8vo. Price 1s. 6d.

Walker (T. H.) *Which is Best? or, Cottage Sketches*
from Real Life. By the Rev. T. H. WALKER. Royal 18mo. Price 2s.

Walker (T. H.) *Gems of Piety in Humble Life.* By the
Rev. T. H. WALKER. Royal 18mo. Price 2s. 6d.

Walker (T. H.) *Youthful Obligations; or, the Duties*
which Young People owe to God, to their Parents, to their Brothers and Sisters, to Themselves, and to Society. Illustrated by a Large Number of Appropriate Facts and Anecdotes. Royal 18mo. Price 2s. 6d.

Watson (R.) *Conversations for the Young.* Designed to
promote the Profitable reading of the Holy Scriptures. Royal 18mo. Price 3s. 6d.

NOW PUBLISHING, IN ROYAL 32MO.

THE METHODIST FAMILY LIBRARY.

	Paper covers. s. d.	Cloth, plain edges. s. d.	Cloth gilt edges. s. d.
THE VOLUMES ALREADY ISSUED ARE:			
1. The Journal of Mr. JOHN NELSON. Written by Himself	6d.	0 10	1 0
2. The Experience and Spiritual Letters of Mrs. HESTER ANN ROGERS	6d.	0 10	1 0
3. Sincere Devotion; Exemplified in the Life of Mrs. MARTIN. By the Rev. B. FIELD	6d.	0 10	1 0
4. The Life of Mr. SILAS TOLD. Written by Himself	6d.	0 10	1 0
5. A Memoir of Mr. WILLIAM CARVOSSO. Sixty Years a Methodist Class-Leader. Written by Himself		1 0	1 4
6. The Life of Mrs. MARY FLETCHER. Written by Himself. Edited by Rev. HENRY MOORE		1 0	1 4
7. The Life of the Rev. JOHN FLETCHER. By the Rev. JOSEPH BENSON		1 0	1 4
8. Prayer: Secret, Social, and Extempore, being a Treatise on Secret and Social Prayer. By the Rev. R. TREFFRY, Sen.; also A HELP TO EXTEMPORE PRAYER. By the Rev. JOSEPH WOOD		1 0	1 4
9. A Memoir of the Rev. DAVID STONER; with Extracts from his Diary and Epistolary Correspondence. By the Rev. JOHN HANNAH and Mr. WILLIAM DAWSON		1 0	1 4
10. Memoirs of the Life, Character, and Labours of the Rev. JOHN SMITH. By the Rev. RICHARD TREFFRY, Jun.		1 0	1 4
11. Entire Sanctification Attainable in this Life; being JOHN WESLEY'S "Plain Account of Christian Perfection," and FLETCHER'S "Practical Application of the Doctrine to various classes of Christians."		1 0	1 4
12. The Pioneer Bishop: The Life and Times of FRANCIS ASBURY. By W. P. STRICKLAND		1 0	1 4
13. A Memoir of JOSEPH B. SHREWSBURY. By his Father, the Rev. W. J. SHREWSBURY		1 0	1 4
14. The Christian Minister in Earnest: A Memoir of the Rev. WILLIAM BRAMWELL. By the Rev. THOMAS HARRIS		1 0	1 4
15. The Life of the Rev. John Wesley, A.M. By the Rev. RICHARD WATSON		1 4	1 9
16. The Life of Dr. Adam Clarke. By J. W. ETHERIDGE, M.A.		1 6	2 0
17. The Life of Dr. Thomas Coke. By J. W. ETHERIDGE, M.A.		1 6	2 0
18. The Life of Dr. Robert Newton. By the Rev. THOMAS JACKSON		1 6	2 0

Complete in Six Volumes, Foolscap 8vo., Cloth, Gilt-lettered,
PRICE EIGHTEENPENCE EACH,

A CHEAP EDITION
OF
LIVES OF
EARLY METHODIST PREACHERS,
WRITTEN CHIEFLY BY THEMSELVES.
EDITED, WITH AN INTRODUCTORY ESSAY, BY THE
REV. THOMAS JACKSON.

CONTENTS OF THE VOLUMES.

VOL. I.—*An Introductory Essay; The Journal of John Nelson: Lives of Christopher Hopper, Thomas Mitchell, Peter Jaco, and John Haime.*

VOL. II.—*Lives of Joseph Cownley, Thomas Olivers, Duncan Wright, Thomas Hanby, Alexander Mather, William Hunter, Robert Roberts, Thomas Payne, and Richard Rodda.*

VOL. III.—*The Life and Death of Mr. Thomas Walsh; and the Lives of John Murlin and John Mason.*

VOL. IV.—*Lives of John Pawson, Sampson Staniforth, Thomas Lee, John Prickard, Jonathan Maskew, Matthias Joyce, and James Rogers.*

VOL. V.—*Lives of Thomas Taylor, John Furz, Thomas Rankin, George Story, William Black, William Ashman, and Richard Whatcoat.*

VOL. VI.—*Lives of John Valton, George Shadford, Jasper Robinson, Thomas Hanson, Robert Wilkinson, Benjamin Rhodes, Thomas Tennant, John Allen, John Pritchard, William Adams;*

AND A GENERAL INDEX TO THE SERIES.

*** *The Library Edition, in Six Volumes, Crown 8vo., on Superfine Paper, is still on sale at 2s. 6d. per Volume.*

"Few lives are more startling than that of John Nelson, few types of saintly holiness are higher than Thomas Walsh; while Thomas Olivers, John Haime, George Story, and Sampson Staniforth, and a number of other goodly names, represent lives of such intense earnestness, holiness, and activity, as would certainly win them a place in a Catholic calendar of saints, and are so full of glowing adventure that the story of many of them would keep a boy's eyes from winking even late in the night."—*British Quarterly Review.*

WESLEYAN CONFERENCE OFFICE,
2, CASTLE-STREET, CITY-ROAD; AND 66, PATERNOSTER-ROW.

www.ingramcontent.com/pod-product-compliance
Lightning Source LLC
Chambersburg PA
CBHW020918230426
43666CB00008B/1493